Jason Has Been Shot!

Jason Has Been Shot!

The True Story of Family, Faith
and the Power of Forgiveness

by **Rev. Dale Lang** and **Mark Lang**

CASTLE QUAY BOOKS
C A N A D A

Jason Has Been Shot!

Copyright © 2003, Castle Quay Books Canada

First printing June 2003
Second printing September 2003

Scripture quotations, unless otherwise indicated, are from the New King James Version. Copyright © 1984, 1982, 1980, 1979. Thomas Nelson Inc., Publishers.

Scriptures marked NIV are from *The Holy Bible, New International Version.* Copyright © 1984, 1978, 1973. International Bible Society. Used by permission of Zondervan Publishing House. All rights reserved.

Cover Design by John Cowie, eyetoeye design
Copy editing by Rick Hiebert
Proofreading by Janet Dimond
Printed by Essence Publishing, Belleville, Ontario

Published by CASTLE QUAY BOOKS
1740 Pilgrim's Way, Oakville, ON L6M 1S5
Tel: (416) 573-3249 Fax: (519) 748-9835
E-mail: info@castlequaybooks.com
www.castlequaybooks.com

National Library of Canada Cataloguing in Publication

Lang, Dale
    Jason has been shot!:the true story of family, faith and the power of forgiveness / Dale Lang.

ISBN 1-894860-20-9

    1. Lang, Dale. 2. Lang, Jason. 3. Forgiveness – Religious aspects – Christianity. 4. Spiritual healing. 5. Parents of murder victims – Alberta – Taber – Biography. 6. Anglican Church of Canada – Clergy – Biography. I. Title.

BX5620.L35A3 2003   241'.4   C2003-902904-2

Table of Contents

Foreword

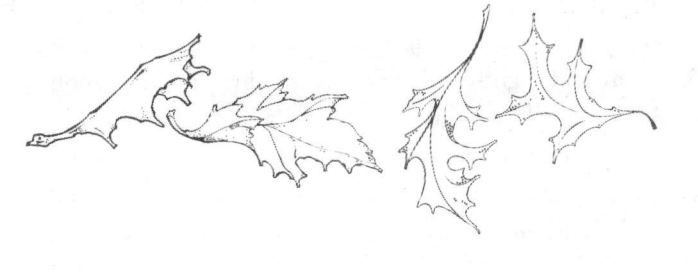

Seven weeks after the murder of Jason Lang, I met Jason's Dad, Mom, brother Mark, other family members, and several members of the Anglican congregation, St. Theodore's. It was a Sunday morning. I had been travelling and living in a van and was in the midst of a 25,000 kilometre prayer pilgrimage across Canada in preparation for the new millennium.

My stop in Taber was a God appointment. The service had just begun as I slipped into a back pew where I was surrounded by young people, including Mark Lang, the son of the rector. Immediately, I was surprised by joy! Dale, an Anglican priest, was leading worship between the altar and the front pews. I actually think I saw the glow of God upon their faces. The worship experience drew me to the heart of God almost irresistibly. Then, with that same authority I had witnessed on prime time newscasts a few days earlier, Dale prayed. O how he prayed! I began to understand why God had enabled Dale to minister to the hurts of millions of Canadians in the days following Jason's tragic death.

I was not surprised to read in The Hon. Preston Manning's new book that he referred to "...the life experience and sufferings of a Václav Havel or a Dale Lang or a Nelson Mandela..." as being such that these men have acquired a national level of "moral authority." Mr. Manning, this former Leader of Her Majesty's Official Opposition in the Parliament of Canada, came to the same conclusion about Dale as have a host of other Canadians.

Currently, Crossroads/100 Huntley Street/CTS is greatly honoured to have Rev. Dale Lang as our daily Bible teacher throughout 2003. Daily and nightly, this minister of Christ pours into our lives as God has poured love, faith, truth, and wisdom into his.

I must warn the reader – you'll never be the same after you've read this book. Be ready to rearrange your priorities, your understanding of pain and tragedy, and the level of your commitment to God.

David Mainse
Former Host, 100 Huntley Street

Preface

Many of you who will read this book have already heard bits of our story. Maybe you remember watching the news that fateful April day in 1999, or maybe you watched the memorial service on television days later. Others may have heard me speak in one of the various places I have travelled. Some of you may not have heard a thing about it, so all this will be new to you. Regardless of what you know or don't know, nobody knows the full story, with the exception of my wife and children. I'm not sure whether it's even possible to get the whole story in one book. I'm not even going to try. I wish to paint a word picture for you. A picture that will show not only that traumatic day and its aftermath, but how we as a family, and more specifically I, got to that point in our lives.

I'm told the reason our situation got so much attention (aside from the obvious) is because there was something different about us. We didn't react in the *normal* or expected way. Well for us there was no other way to react, and my hope for this book is that it will explain why. I also hope it will impact you personally. I wouldn't have written it otherwise.

I don't have some narcissistic need to tell our story just for the sake of telling it. History is something we should learn from, though far too often we simply ignore and repeat it. This story is now part of our history, and because of the national attention it received it's a significant part of many others' as well. We need to learn from it. I hope after reading this book you will understand how we can change things, rather than simply be doomed to repeat our most evil, foolish veins of history.

I would like to particularly challenge you to really examine things beyond, shall we say, a simply physical or natural reality. I believe the main reason we have been doomed to repeat our mistakes throughout history is simply because we don't see the spiritual root of the original problems. In fact, we don't even consider it most of the time. So inevitably we think we can avoid the same outcome if we do things a little differently – but we haven't changed the real problem and almost always lose the battle. The medical field is an unpleasantly conspicuous microcosm of this principle. We so frequently treat the symptoms and are unable to treat or cure the root problem. I learned this painfully well through my son Mark (whom you'll read about later). We try to control unpleasant symptoms as long as possible, but far too often the root problem wins with time.

Inevitably, telling our story is simply telling a story about God and our relationships with Him. Please don't get this confused with religion. The two are very, very different. I haven't to this day even once tried to exclude God from the story, a story I have shared in hundreds of public schools, conventions, businesses and even in Parliament to some degree. Even if I could exclude Him, which I can't, I wouldn't want to. You see the story is about the unseen versus the seen, infinite things versus finite things. There simply is no story without God – none! If you don't believe in God, fine. Don't let that stop you from reading this book. It may still have something to say to you. If you're mad at Him, well, He's a big God, He can take it. Don't let that stop you from reading either. In the end this story is about things that either do or soon will affect everybody. My prayer for this book is that it will challenge you to look at yourself and society from a different perspective.

April 28, 1999

Waves of nausea swept through my stomach as I hung up the phone. Pale, I turned to Diane and shared with her what had been said. We headed out the door for the hospital blanketed by a cloud of confusion and fear. In the small town of Taber it is only a five-minute drive to the hospital. That short drive still seemed an eternity as we wondered together what could have gone wrong and how *serious* was serious? Jason had purchased a used car just two days earlier and I was fearful that he might have been involved in a car accident. I couldn't fathom anything else having gone wrong.

We pulled into the hospital parking lot as that low, grey sky started to release a few drops of rain. Rushing into the emergency unit of our hospital we were met at the door by the person who had called.

He greeted us with those unforgettable words: "Jason has been *shot*"...

Hot Air and the Call

I guess this story really starts on August 18, 1951 in Calgary, Alberta. It was a hot summer day in the city. On that day I, Dale Frederick Lang, was born. Then, the following year, in the month of May, Barbara Diane McMurray was born, and so our story had begun. Here's where I'll fast-forward my story, because no one needs to read the mundane details of another normal childhood. Suffice to say I was raised in a loving home with one pain-in-the-neck sister (whom I love) and two wonderful parents. After graduating from high school, which delighted me greatly, and spending some time milling around, I had embarked on what I thought would be the best life possible.

At the end of high school I started dating the aforementioned Diane McMurray and sparks flew. Even then my immature teenage mind recognized that this was going to be one of the best and most important decisions of my life. In 1972 she consented to be my wife. Two years later I came across another important opportunity. It came in the form of a bag filled with hot air, or so to speak. It all started one fall morning in 1973. Diane and I got out of bed early that Saturday morning, no particular reason. Out of mere curiosity we went down to Riley Park in Calgary to watch some hot air balloons fly. Even as a young kid the idea of flying in a balloon had captured my imagination. That chilly October morning would prove to be a significant turn in the road of my life. Mesmerized, I watched as those lifeless bags of fabric expanded into dancing rainbows and finally colourful floating bubbles that were effortlessly and gently drifting away. I was hooked and I thought to myself, I have got to fly one of these things.

It wasn't going to be enough for me to just go for a ride. I was really hooked. So a few months later, without ever having even flown in one, I obtained a bank loan (it always helps to have your wife working in a bank). I used the money to purchase a used balloon and pilot training from a rather colourful fellow in Coeur d'Alene, Idaho. I will never forget my first flight. I had been down in Idaho for a couple of weeks waiting for suitable flying weather. The weather seemed to be mocking me as day after agonizing day went by without flyable conditions. Finally that day arrived, a sunny early spring afternoon and the winds were *light*. Gordon, my instructor, chose a highway rest stop as our launch site. This rest stop was just outside of Coeur d'Alene on the highway heading over to Spokane, Washington. It was a beautiful spot surrounded by tall pines. I had been anticipating this moment for so long I wondered if I might have set myself up for disappointment. Before I knew it the balloon was filled with air and Gordon had turned on the burners. The bag began to rise in response to the heat. In short order the balloon was upright and ready to fly.

We lifted off that day in near calm conditions. I can still remember as we slowly moved upward, clearing the tops of those pines. A beautiful view of the whole valley emerged as we ascended higher. In retrospect I now realize that my fate was sealed in those first thirty seconds of flight. It was even better than I had ever imagined. Eventually I returned home with the balloon and a license to fly. I would spend the next ten years building and running my own hot air balloon business in Calgary. Looking back on those times I can only say that I enjoyed those years immensely, which of course made the coming changes even more extraordinary.

Life is a strange adventure filled with irony. I can remember turning forty-five in 1996 and saying to Diane that if I were to die that night I would have nothing to complain about. My life had been filled with immense blessings and wonderful opportunities – very few tragedies littered the roadside. Looking back, I suppose that should have made me wonder what was to come, but it didn't. People seem to spend a lot of time trying to figure out what will happen in the future – but for the most part we are better off not knowing.

Happy Times
Are Not Enough

In the mid-1970s it seemed to me that life couldn't get a whole lot better. The economy in Canada, and specifically Alberta, was going through unprecedented prosperity. I was consumed with my little hot air balloon business, enjoying my marriage, and living a fairly happy life. I saw no need for any changes other than the usual Canadian complaint that I could have used more money. I guess you could say I was happy.

The balloon business was growing well, despite the misgivings of family and friends who thought I was crazy trying to turn this pastime into a business. How many people are able to get up early every morning looking forward to the day's work? Flying balloons, from that very first flight right up to the present, has been a passion for me; I just love it. I didn't think it was too crazy to make a living from something I loved. My life was very comfortable, and in my experience, whenever you come to a situation like that, change is already on the horizon. At that point in my life though, I sure didn't foresee the imminent changes that were hanging over my head, and thankfully wouldn't have been able to stop them anyway.

The first pending change was on the day in 1976 that Diane told me she was pregnant. I didn't think I was ready for parenthood, not even close. We always knew we wanted to have children but there were so many unknowns. Specifically, I was in the midst of building a small business and the timing seemed less than appropriate to me.

My initial surprise and concern about the birth of our first child faded quickly. Soon we began to look forward to the arrival of a new little person to our family. The expected arrival date was early May, 1977. Time seemed to pass me by somewhere in the business of life, and before I knew it 1976 had morphed into 1977. April of that year was a busy time for me at work. We had been contracted to take a balloon to the Arctic. The oil company Phoenix Ventures had hired us. They wanted to use one of our balloons as a visual platform to scout ice conditions for their exploration work.

Making the trek up to Resolute Bay, and then on to the polar ice cap to work with them about the middle of April, I was only scheduled to be there for two weeks. Then Mr. Bruce Bailey, who was working for me at that time, would take over. This plan had been arranged so I could be home for the birth of our baby. Of course the best-laid plans and the arrival of babies don't always coincide. On April 28, shortly after Bruce had arrived to take my place, word came across our base camp radio that Diane had given birth to our first son. In all honesty at first I didn't believe that message. The East Indian fellow who operated the radio was a practical joker and I thought he was playing another prank. Not only that, I very clearly remember telling Diane that she was to wait until I got home to have the baby, and I was quite serious, you know.

It took some prodding but the folks at the base camp finally convinced me of the truth – I had a son. I remember walking away from camp, slightly overwhelmed. In the Arctic when you get away from other people you find yourself engulfed by a deafening silence.

Nothing seems to stir on that peaceful ice. If you listen for a while you can actually hear your own heart beating. On that day, standing in silence, I looked out across the vast expanse. It was brilliant, even radiant, this frozen ocean awash in the perpetual Arctic sunlight. In that moment something changed. It was a new realization that came in the form of a thought. It came to me in an unusual way as though someone else was talking to me: "There is more to life than you realize, Dale. There is more to life than you can see with your eyes." It seemed to echo endlessly along the barren landscape, gliding along the ice. At first I just put it aside, trying to rationalize it by reasoning that I was overwhelmed. I have found that this is one of life's great struggles – the compelling drive to make sense of anything we don't understand with terms (however inaccurate or inadequate) we do understand. It was three days later in the Foothills Hospital in Calgary when I first saw our son, Jeff. My brain had discreetly tucked the thought away in the "explained file," but it came back powerfully as I looked upon my son. However, once again I would file this "impression" away. After all, I was living my happy life now even more complete with our newborn son. What else could I need?

Baby Times

Those first few months with Jeff were amazing. I remember saying to Diane at one point, "What did we ever do before the baby came?" My level of happiness was noticeably growing. Life for me was an adventure and it just kept getting better. I was sort of making a living by flying balloons and I enjoyed our new son immensely. Things were great. A dangerous place to be if you remember what I said earlier. My old friend *change* was knocking at the door yet again. This time he came in the form of a conversation with Diane. Before a word even sprang from her lips I could tell that this was going to be important. She had that look on her face, and it definitely wasn't going to be a discussion about what to have for dinner. Diane had been raised in the Anglican church, and as is very common, the miracle of birth had stirred her spirit. She wanted Jeff to be baptized. Her Anglican background told her that it was very important. In hindsight it seems rather humorous that a bad piece of theology would be used by God to touch our lives. From her church experience Diane believed you had to be baptized to get into Heaven.

My response to this was guarded. I had been raised in a loving family but my parents had, for a number of reasons, rejected the church. After thinking it over I couldn't see any harm in the situation. Even though the idea meant nothing to me I had no basis to object, so I relented. "If it makes you feel good, that's fine. Just remember it means nothing to me." The look on Diane's face seemed to intensify even a little bit more. Then with a little apprehension she asked me another question: "Well," she said, "I know you haven't been baptized either, so I would like you to be baptized at the same time, too." Diane's logic was that if she was going to Heaven, I had better be going as well. Putting aside my discomfort, I saw no valid reason to object. I thought if this is going to please her, then why not? "Okay, but just remember it doesn't mean anything to me. I'm just doing it for you."

So in the fall of 1977 Jeff and I, one as clueless as the other, were baptized. There was a tiny chapel built by her family on their acreage west of Calgary. It was there in that quaint setting with much of our family gathered around that it took place. Ironically, the minister baptized Jeff and almost forgot about me. Years later I would find out that Diane's father had said to her that afternoon, "Watch Dale now. The Holy Spirit has come into his life in a new way and he will start asking questions."

The impact of that earlier Arctic thought was still creating ripples in my soul. The baptism had also churned my curiosity more than I had initially expected. So I embarked on a search to see if there was some ultimate truth to life. Over the next several months I began asking questions. I started reading books of all kinds exploring different perspectives on the meaning of life. Through this time Diane's dad, Norm, was there to answer some of my questions. He had spent roughly ten years studying different religions and philosophies. By the end of his search he had returned to Christianity.

Through my searching I had begun to read some of the New Testament. One particular fellow, namely Jesus, had begun to intrigue me. I just couldn't figure Him out, and believe me I tried.

None of the normal human motives seemed to be present in Him. He wasn't chasing after personal glory, I saw no greed, and in fact, in the end it would be His incredible self-giving love that would convince me of who He really was.

Little did I realize that I was about to make the most profound life-altering, foundation-shaking decision of my short life. We were visiting Diane's family one day. I can still remember it clearly. I was enthralled by a popular Christian book of the time. I excused myself to the throne room and sitting there, continued to read the book. At the end of the chapter I was reading, the author simply asked a question. He asked if wasn't it time I entered into a relationship with Jesus? It was kind of funny because as I read the words on the page it was more like someone was verbally asking me that question. At that precise moment I knew without a shadow of a doubt that Jesus was the answer to life. I finally grasped the dramatic difference between religion and relationship with Jesus, the difference between the Church (as an organization) and Christianity. Sitting there that very day I followed the little prayer laid out in the book and I entered into a relationship with Jesus. Of course I had no idea at the time what that would really mean. Somehow I just knew it was right.

It's probably not possible to take God too seriously. Much of the time we take ourselves far too seriously, and often miss the Lord's incredible sense of humour. Just imagine this picture: a guy who was incredibly happy with his life. He had been baptized as a confessing *non*-believer only because of his wife's improper understanding of baptism. To top it all off, he committed his life to Jesus while sitting on a toilet reading a book that he now considers pretty poor theology. You just have to laugh when you really think about it. I have often found Church people way too stuffy. If you look closely you can see that God has an amazing sense of humour. He created us in His image – we can have that good sense of humour, too.

Turning from Happiness to Joy

There was a lot of happiness in my life directly preceding my foray into Christianity. Looking back, it strikes me as all the more amazing that I would even take the time to consider God. People who are fairly happy with their lives are not keen on rocking the boat. Often they are the most difficult people to talk to about the things of God. I think it's safe to say that generally people who are comfortable want to stay that way.

The first year of my life as a Christian was a strange time. Diane and I had attended an Anglican church periodically but I found the experience boring. It had no positive impact on my life. During that year some friends, whom we had met in a marriage preparation course back in 1972, moved back to Calgary from the Okanagan Valley in British Columbia. In the time they were away they had also become Christians. Diane and I began to meet with them once a week for an informal Bible study. During this time Diane also became a Christian. Even though she was raised in the Anglican Church she had never been clearly taught that Christianity was a relationship, not a religion.

During those months that little Bible study kept me enthused about my relationship with Jesus. Very slowly we began to grow in our understanding of what this was all about, and what it meant to have relationship with Jesus as opposed to intellectual knowledge of Him. Our friends in the Bible study, Paul and Marg, were attending a different Anglican church. Perhaps the word different is a bit under-stated – maybe incredibly understated would be more accurate. They began telling us about this church and our curiosity grew until it finally overtook us.

Entering St. James that first Sunday was an eye-opening experience. Unlike other churches I had been in, there was excitement in the air. People were very welcoming and friendly and there was an anticipation that important, life-changing things were about to happen. It put a whole new definition on the word "church," as far as we knew anyway. That Sunday morning would be another momentous changing point in our lives. For me, it is second only to the actual day of my decision to become a Christian. It wasn't just some boring, dry service with rules and regulations. It was alive with the breath of God. It was much closer to what I had read about in the Bible. We became members of St. James Church shortly thereafter, and this would be the place where God would begin the process of truly changing us as people.

Those first few years at St. James brought us into a whole new experience of God. In this church they *actually* believed that Jesus would heal people, and many were. At the heart of the whole thing was a rather simple and Biblical teaching. It was the idea of opening up your life to allow the Holy Spirit to empower you as a disciple of Jesus. Those days in our lives were days of adventure and growth.

Again time seemed to slip away from me, and before I knew what had happened our second son, Mark, arrived on the scene. Mark was very unlike his older brother Jeff. Jeff was a content little fellow, cautious of the world. Mark, on the other hand, was bold and seemed to fear nothing. This would lead to many family adventures.

I can remember one such time when Jeff and Mark were playing in the schoolyard across the street from where we lived. In that schoolyard there was a steep little hill. The two boys had gone over there with Jeff's bicycle and Mark's tricycle. They came to the edge of the daunting hill as we watched from our living room window. We kept saying, "They won't try riding their bikes down that hill." Oh, what famous last words. After a brief conversation between the two boys, and before we could move, Mark was heading down the hill, smile and all. It wasn't long before he had to take his feet off the pedals as they spun wildly out of control. Before arriving at the bottom, the inevitable wipeout took place. All the while we watched helplessly from the house. Mark was okay, not even a tear, but Jeff decided he didn't need to try it. Thus was set in place a pattern that would occur over and over again. Mark would try everything first. If he survived, Jeff might dare to try. It still amazes me how every child that comes along is so unique from all the others in the family.

A Life-Long Connection to Teenagers

Time continued to press forward and before I knew it, I found myself working with youth. One particular memory surfaces rather clearly. It was a quieter ride than many I had taken with a vanload of teenagers. We left Calgary around 9 a.m. that sunny morning heading for Drumheller, Alberta, and the land of bones – dinosaur bones to be specific. It was the spring of 1984 and I had been involved in youth ministry at St. James Anglican Church for four years.

This particular trip had been spawned by the teens having a day off school. It would not be the last youth event that I would organize, but I remember it specifically because that familiar feeling of change was already in the air. The van was loaded with eight or nine teenagers plus my two oldest sons, Jeff (seven) and Mark (five). Sarah and Wendy were among the kids there. These two girls were very close friends. It was always enjoyable to have them along because they were always, always laughing about something. There was Dave and Steve who had become good friends in the youth group. Losing his dad five years earlier had been extremely difficult for Steve, and the sense of community brought by the group was a good thing for him. On the other hand, Dave had joined the group at the insistence of his parents. Like any responsible parents, they were concerned for Dave because of the destructive path he seemed to be navigating, so they plugged him in with us. The two had become fast friends and were nearly inseparable at youth group events.

In the midst of this collection of kids was a young man who was relatively new to our group. His name was Carl. He was a nice enough kid, but from the moment I laid eyes on him I knew he had gone through some tough times. He was one of those kids who stood out as being a little different, which meant that he would not always fit in socially with others. A different sense of humour, not being dressed in the latest "cool styles," and his reactions all revealed that some of his peers had not been too kind along the way.

The kids in our group had accepted Carl fairly well. Sarah and Wendy, having gone through some ridicule themselves, had a wonderful sensitivity to others who were hurting and made sure Carl felt welcome. For the most part, our group of kids knew that we supported and encouraged anyone who came out, as a reflection of God's love.

After we arrived we spent the day touring the museum and wandering about the always fascinating rock formations known as "hoodoos." The weather was nice and we had a good time in Drumheller. Everything had gone well on this lazy, laid-back day and everyone enjoyed it, junk food and all. It would be that junk food, however, that would create a *situation*. It turned out that Carl had consumed perhaps more than his fair share of snacks. About twenty minutes out of Drumheller on the way home, Carl, who was sitting quietly in the first bench seat behind me, abruptly threw up without any forewarning. This kind of moment is embarrassing for anyone, but of course in those teen years everything is magnified by raging hormones and newly forming social skills.

We pulled off onto the side of the highway where Carl completed his vomiting. Of course, being the well-organized, prepared-for-anything youth pastor, I had nothing to clean up the mess. The only option was another ten minutes of driving until we got to a service station. Naturally the group made all the expected comments during that ten-minute drive. Carl was still looking a little green, and I certainly felt for him. Why is it that the kids who have a harder time fitting in usually end up in these situations? In the end we all survived this minor ordeal, and looking back, it's those quirky stories I remember the most. Carl was just one of many hurting young people I have had the privilege of working with over the last twenty years. It seems more than a bit ironic that after having cared for so many young people, many of them damaged from life issues, that one such young man would end up being the cause of the deepest pain of my life.

I remember the day very clearly when the Lord recruited me to enter the world of teenagers. Diane and I, as mentioned previously, had been attending St. James Anglican Church in Calgary. Even though I had been a Christian for nearly two years, it was in the lively atmosphere of this church in renewal where my life would take some incredible turns.

In the few months we had spent at this *unusual* Anglican church, God had developed in me a desire to be doing something for Him. It was primarily through the preaching and teaching of Rev. Charles Alexander that this desire was sparked and fanned. I knew that there was so much more than just being in the pew on Sunday morning. One particular Sunday after the service was over, I just happened to be passing Charles in the foyer of the church. He looked up as we crossed paths and before we were even a few steps apart he paused, looked back, and said, "Have you ever considered working with teenagers? I just have this sense that maybe the Lord is calling you to ministry with the youth." I looked blankly at Charles and said, "Sure, whatever the Lord wants is fine with me."

I remember walking away from that brief divine encounter, exhilarated. There was a place of ministry in the church for me! An hour or so later, after arriving home and actually thinking about what I had agreed to, I don't think it's exaggerating to say that I went into shock. What? Me work with teenagers? I didn't even like teenagers! They hung around in herds, they always made smart-mouth remarks, they were not friendly people. In the end, with much fear and trepidation, I entered this foreign land of acne and hormones, praying that I might survive.

My first youth job was to run a Bible study for junior high school kids on Sunday mornings during the church service. There was one snag with this situation. St. James was in a fast-growing area of Calgary and the church was full. On top of that, the building had been designed without a lot of vision and all this translated into no space to meet with these young people. Thankfully, a wonderful couple from the church, John Torley and his wife Lil, (who would later be called and ordained to a very fruitful ministry themselves) lived across the street and graciously allowed us to meet in their unfinished basement.

It would be an understatement to say those early youth days were trying times. I must have made every mistake in the book, and invented a few new ones, too. In the end there was one thing that saved me – the love. My enthusiasm made up for my vast lack of both wisdom and knowledge, and that enthusiasm was a gift from God. More importantly, it took very little time for me to begin to love these young people and care about their lives. I discovered, contrary to my previous stereotypical view, that these kids were wonderful young people. Yes, many of them came with baggage. Yet God's love growing in me made it possible for me to see just how precious they all were. These early shaky beginnings would eventually, by the grace of the Lord, turn into a ministry that would touch a couple hundred young lives in the four years we were there. Even today I still see or speak to many of those young people who now have their own children. God used these young people to teach me and help me along the road to maturity. These were the building blocks I would so desperately need later on in life.

The Journey of Joy

Those earlier years of children being born were so incredibly rich. Many of us are so busy in those times, building careers and growing families, that we aren't always aware of just how amazing and how short that time is. For me, this time in my life had been even more extraordinary as I became a Christian and entered into a relationship with Jesus. This new relationship had taken me from a self-centred place of mainly seeking my own happiness, and had deposited me on a foundation of joy and peace, something I had never experienced before. I'm not saying that my life was perfect, but underlying all the emotional ups and downs was that foundation, sturdy and unwavering. The Lord was changing me from the inside out, a process that continues to this day. I was actually able to put the needs of others before myself. I always thought that I was a good and moral person, but this was very different. Looking back on those years, I am thankful to God for that because it helped me to stop all my busyness, at least long enough to take some time and enjoy my children while they were little.

The year 1982 would again plant seeds of change as we drew near to the next major shift in our lives. February 27 was the date of arrival for our third son, Jason. Once again I would learn that every person is unique. Jason was a fairly quiet little fellow, a trait that would mark the rest of his life. I remember Diane remarking that she had a deep sense of the Lord's presence when he was born, something that she would remember and treasure when 1999 came along.

During the summer of that year St. James sent us to Bath, Ohio to St. Luke's Episcopal Church. This particular church was a leading church in renewal and their youth pastor, Wally Schilling, was running a three-month course on youth ministry. The congregation of St. Luke's was filled with wonderful, passionate people. We were the only married couple in the course, and obviously the only ones with children. This presented a minor problem as all the other students were being housed in a modest dorm-like facility. The problem was solved when a gracious older couple in the church took us into their home for the three-month period. A bold step when you consider the two small boys and a baby.

Those three months were used by God to bring us yet closer to Him. The congregation treated us like any other member of the family and we felt right at home. I remember driving out of Bath when that course was over, tears running down my face as we were leaving. We had made so many incredible friends whom we had come to love and it was difficult to go.

Looking back, I can see so clearly how the impact of that summer in Bath watered and nurtured the seeds of change. Upon returning to St. James I had a deepening hunger to serve the Lord, and I felt called to be doing more in the church. This idea manifested itself in my desire to be employed full-time as a youth worker. St. James had already decided to pay me a part-time wage but I really wanted to be doing this work full-time. In those days, full-time youth workers in the Anglican Church were scarce to say the least, and the prospects were not good.

At the same time in Canada, Prime Minister Trudeau had introduced his controversial Energy Bill, which was turning Alberta's boom days into bust. For me personally this caused a sharp decline in our thriving hot air balloon business. The winds of change were beginning to increase, driving us toward destiny. My enjoyment of flying balloons had not wavered. However the challenges of running a business under the mounting pressure of Alberta's bust days was not my heart's desire. There is no doubt that we were quickly arriving at a crossroads in our lives.

By this time we had been living in a side-by-side duplex with our friends Paul and Marg Viergutz. We had put a door in the basement between the two sides. We did this because we wanted to live in a type of Christian community. We had dinner together at least once a week and met and prayed together at least once a week as well. All through this time Paul and Marg were there supporting us, and it meant a lot.

Eventually I started to notice a peculiar comment that was coming up in conversations with a variety of people. This reoccurring comment was something like: "Maybe you should think about becoming ordained." Let's be clear. Initially this idea held no attraction for me at all – none. I believe that lay people are called to ministry just like those who are ordained. I loved what I was doing and to top it off, I had found many clergy to be a bit stuffy and boring. I just couldn't see myself in such a role. Yet those comments kept coming and eventually I felt that I should at least look into the possibility.

Before taking the plunge and talking to our bishop, I said one prayer: "Lord if You want me to do this, You will have to open all the doors because if even one closes I will not go." It is always dangerous to lay such prayers before God. In short, several hurdles had to be overcome for me to be accepted and before it would be possible to go to seminary. Often this process takes two years. Within a six-month time frame I had all of the necessary approvals and we were heading for Ambridge, Pennsylvania, toward another amazing adventure.

Three Years on Faith

During the time of preparation for this next huge shift in our lives, we felt God calling us to attend a new seminary in the United States. There were schools much closer to us in Canada that we could have attended, but there was this undeniable tug toward Ambridge. In the Anglican Church, such decisions are made in consultation with the sponsoring bishop. I went to meet with Bishop Barry Curtis about this issue and I was surprised that he happily agreed to allow us to study at Trinity Episcopal School for Ministry.

The spring of 1984 greeted us with the birth of our fourth son, Matthew. We were right in the middle of preparations to make the trek into the waiting foreign land. Matthew would certainly provide another change in our family. Even from his early days, we could see that this fellow had a definite and strong mind of his own. I was rather poorly equipped for the challenges of helping a guy, who may just be more stubborn than I am, to stay on track. Even though I didn't know it at the time, there would be many frustrating times ahead with this gifted but very obstinate lad. Early on, Matthew provided many interesting times as he wandered the neighbourhood in Sewickley, often with a diaper hanging down around his knees.

As you can imagine, this was not quite the ideal situation. Three small boys and one brand new baby made this move very challenging. During one particularly intense and frustrating moment, Diane suggested I should go alone as she waited in Canada.

Despite all the fear and trepidation, somewhere in the middle of August, we set out on the open highway, headed for Western Pennsylvania. Our extended van was packed to the gills and was closely followed by a rented trailer. It proved to be a three-and-a-half-day journey. We would make this drive a total of six times over the next three years. All six times we made that trek safely and had a good time doing it. Those three years in Pittsburgh will always be, for me, some of the very best times of my life.

I must admit that the studies were challenging for a guy in his mid-thirties who never had much interest in academics. My saving grace was that I was highly motivated and surprisingly enjoyed the stretching of so many brain cells. The school was small, allowing the faculty and student body to pull together as a very real Christian community to help and support one another. In Ambridge I had only two things to focus on – my studies and my family. It was a great time and I actually stayed well organized, something new for me. I got my studies done and spent a lot of time with the family.

Looking back on those days, I know God blessed us in so many incredible ways, but perhaps the most amazing thing was our finances. Every year we would journey back to Calgary where I had one hot air balloon advertising contract left with the Coca-Cola Corporation. This allowed me to continue flying and also brought in our only source of income. It provided only 40 percent of the money we needed each year to attend school. Yet amazingly, for those three years, we never ran out of money. We were never lacking anything we needed. Sometimes it would look like we were in trouble and out of the blue someone would send us a cheque in the mail.

One day I remember driving from Sewickley, the town where we rented a house, to the school in Ambridge (a three-mile drive). I was listening to the radio and the news came on. The newsman reported that Michael Jackson's latest album (*Thriller*) had made several million dollars in just three weeks. I remember a surge of anger coursing through my body. I said, "God, why does someone who doesn't need any money get so much and we lowly students trying to serve You have so little?" This was one of those moments when the Lord spoke very clearly and immediately to my mind. He said, "Tell me what it is that you are lacking?" Driving down the road that day, I just shrivelled in my seat and weakly responded, "Nothing." It was true. For the entire three years we never missed a meal or anything else for that matter. Even more incredible to me was that we never incurred one cent of debt. Debt is something so many of us struggle with in today's world, and sadly I have been no exception. I could write a whole other book on debt, but during those three years we were completely and absolutely debt free. God is always more amazing than most of us ever realize.

I truly enjoyed my studies and time at Trinity School for Ministry. We forged life-long friendships that we know will stretch into eternity. But by far the greatest blessing of that time was our family. We didn't have money to do much, but we spent wonderful times together. Probably one of my greatest joys was our bike rides. Jeff and Mark, the two oldest boys, had their own bikes while Di and I had those little white children's seats mounted on the back of our bikes. Di would have our youngest, Matthew, behind her and I would have Jason behind me. Each of them was strapped in and wearing those little white helmets that were available in those days.

Sewickley was built on a plateau above the river and was relatively flat. We would go out on a fall evening and cruise the streets, pushing through the sweet, warm, and humid air. Each street was walled with the incredibly vibrant colours of changing leaves on the hardwood trees. Nestled behind the bastion of trees were stately century-old houses. If those houses could have talked they would have entertained us for hours with interesting tales. They had once been the summer getaway homes of the wealthy steel families from Pittsburgh. Many of those rides ended up at Friendly's restaurant down by the river for ice cream. I think if there was ever a time I wanted to freeze life and stay in a moment forever, that was it.

A New Life in the Middle of Somewhere

The spring of '87 snuck up on us and popped the little bubble we had been living in. It brought with it a mixed blessing – graduation and a permanent return to the Anglican Diocese of Calgary. We knew it was time to move ahead, even though that meant leaving behind our many wonderful friendships and a time-rich family environment. I can't overstate how wonderful our family life was there and I will never stop thanking the Lord for it. Returning to Calgary and being ordained as a deacon was the natural outcome of the theological training, and yet it had very minimal meaning for me. I was anxious to get involved in the ministry I had been trained for. I wanted to see people's lives healed by the transforming love of Jesus. I felt titles were simply cumbersome and often used politically.

I couldn't help but spend some time in my last year pondering where we might end up. I watched the newsletters to see what churches were in need of clergy. Where we were about to end up had never appeared on any lists. After returning to Calgary, the Bishop asked us to go to this place called Taber, and do an interview. I had never been to Taber. I knew it was a small town down south and not much more. The southernmost reaches of Alberta had always struck me as depressing. Dry, semi-arid land with a lot of wind and almost no trees. It was hardly my idea of a great place to live. I could accept almost anything but that wind. I had no intentions of giving up balloon piloting just because I was a pastor now. I remember the drive down the evening we were to be interviewed by the parish. Another Anglican priest, Derek Hoskins, was driving us from his church in Fort Macleod to Taber. I looked out over the open fields and thought, "Lord, this isn't very appealing. You don't really want us here, do you?"

Finally driving into the town of Taber, I felt a little relief wash over me. The townsite itself contained a lot of trees and even though it was a small place, it didn't look all that bad. The really good news was that it was a half-hour drive from the small city of Lethbridge. This proximity to Lethbridge would be one of the main factors that made it bearable to live in Taber for several years. Shortly after we arrived, Diane and I met with the interview committee. We enjoyed a lovely home-cooked meal and talked with the folks throughout supper. Then we went through an hour interview where the ten or twelve people took turns asking us questions. God had given me a peace about doing interviews because I knew that He had picked out the place where He wanted us to be. This removed any pressure to "sell" myself. It was very liberating to know in my spirit that it was out of my hands, and it was easy for me to be honest about the call on my life and how I felt the Lord was leading me.

During the interview process committee members shared where they thought they were headed and what they needed. Later I would realize that much of what they said was said because it seemed like the *right* thing to want. In the midst of all this discussion, the folks also revealed that they had gone through a very difficult time with their last rector. The situation had ended badly with dissension in the congregation. The bishop had been forced to finally ask for the rector's resignation. They then hastened to add that they felt the necessity of an experienced priest to help them move ahead.

The journey back to Calgary that night was one of peace. Both Diane and I felt that the interview had gone very well but I didn't believe we would be going there. After all, we had just come out of school and they really emphasized their need for healing. I felt on that basis alone they would pass us by for someone with more experience. Some two weeks later word came to us from the bishop that we had been unanimously called to go to Taber. I was a bit surprised but we did not question the decision or God. We moved to Taber at the end of August to begin the next leg of our journey with Jesus. When we take Him seriously and let Him drive, there is one thing I can say without a doubt – life is never, never boring.

People, Patience and Persistence

Starting a new phase of life when you are full of enthusiasm and have numerous challenges to attack really is an adventure. I went into Taber full of faith and desiring to see God move mountains. The church of St. Theodore's Taber was at that time a *very* traditional Anglican church with 70 percent of the active parishioners over 60 years of age. There was no one in the church between the ages of 16 and 30. The task was formidable, and if I knew then what I know now, I may not have made it through to this point in time.

The people of St. Theodore's welcomed us and made us feel comfortable. Like most traditional congregations, what they really wanted was the old stereotypical chaplain – someone who would preach a good sermon (that means interesting or entertaining), be able to communicate with teenagers, and visit the older folks. Generally people in these circumstances will tolerate anything you might want to do as long as it doesn't disturb their comfort zone.

It had to be God because I was sure they had the wrong guy. I was not particularly worried about any traditional limitations. I had been involved in the renewal of the church now for some nine years. God was giving me a vision for a renewed, passionately-on-fire-for-Him church, where there was life and life-changing opportunities. A place where people not only thought about God but experienced Him in a very tangible way. In other words, a church of action. Yet once again the Lord would direct me to walk in grace. Beyond all my own personal capabilities, He allowed me to have patience, moving through what was ahead with joy.

One of the first sermons I preached in St. Theodore's laid the foundation for what I believed God was asking me to do. I was to preach the Word, to help bring to life the reality of a relationship with Jesus. Second, I was to love these people with all my heart. Little did I know at the time how challenging that could be. Third, I was to be a person of prayer. Today I would confess that I certainly have not done all three of these as faithfully as I would have liked. But even in my weak times, Jesus has shone through, revealing just how faithful and unchanging He is.

I could fill several chapters with the adventures and misadventures we experienced during the fifteen years at St. Theodore's. Through it all God was so faithful to us. With a humble heart I can only say I am both blessed and amazed. During those years the Lord changed hearts and ruptured many religious traditions at their foundations. Today they are a congregation that spans all age ranges. Worship is still lively and very centred on Jesus. We saw people healed both physically and emotionally. We have seen numbers of people come to faith. Through it all, God built us into a family where people know they are loved and cared for. I would not have traded that time for anything. Jesus, time and again, revealed His amazing faithfulness to us and has continued to teach us and stretch us. We are not perfect. We will never be in this life, and while we have a long way to grow, God has brought us miles.

A Little Girl Completed It All

After having four sons in a row Diane and I felt that we had a complete family. The four boys were a joy to watch grow, even with their challenges. We were busy with our lives in Taber, and by 1990 all the boys were in school and everything seemed right with our little world.

The church continued to present challenges, yet we saw little victories here and there. I remember a series of congregational meetings where we talked about vision. It was difficult for most of the older folks, who were very set in their ways and saw no need for change. They didn't understand that the way in which we presented the truth of Jesus to the world needed to change. It needed to be relevant. (Don't confuse this with the message changing – the message can't change.)

At one meeting the matriarch of the parish simply sat at the back looking very, very unhappy. I waited a couple of days and then phoned her to see how she was doing. Her response was revealing: "I know things have to change. It's just that everything keeps changing and I really don't want the church to change." I appreciated her honest response. She knew it had to happen but it was hard for her. Shortly after that she became ill with cancer.

The year 1992 proved to be a very challenging one indeed. A couple's twenty-one-year-old son died suddenly one night of a heart attack. Tragically this occurred only months after his uncle had died of leukemia. Another young man I had ministered to for several years who had come to faith, also died that spring after a long-term battle with MS. Adding to the mounting death toll, the matriarch of the church would also succumb to cancer in the spring of that year. Yet in the midst of a dark time, God brought light.

In the fall of 1991 we discovered, much to our shock, that Diane was pregnant. We thought our family was complete and were taking the necessary precautions to avoid such a possibility. Thankfully God's wisdom is always better than ours and always wins in the end. My initial reaction was disbelief, which then progressed to embarrassment before finally reaching its final destination of resignation. I remember it took us both at least a month to come to peace about this little development. Of course, eventually we had to tell our children and then the church. Many of our parishioners were excited about this prospect. We, too, began to accept our fate and eventually began to believe this was a blessing from God.

In the midst of these black days of 1992 we had our fifth child. I remember before I was married teasing my mother that I would have five children and make sure that they spent plenty of time with their grandparents. Of course I never really meant it, but God was obviously listening and I never heard the end of it.

Eventually the fateful day arrived for Diane to give birth. We were all ready to welcome our fifth son into the world. After having four boys it just wasn't possible to believe that we could have a daughter. Several people had said we were going to have a little girl but that's not what we expected. The memory of that day in the delivery room is vividly etched in my mind. I was holding Di's hand when the baby finally emerged, and I heard the doctor say, "It's a girl." Diane immediately looked up at the doctor and said, "You're kidding!" Well, the doctor wasn't kidding and now we faced another shock. After four boys, a little girl.

It took no time at all for us to welcome the new addition into our lives. We knew then that our family was truly complete. Of course nobody warned us just how different little girls can be from little boys. Everybody seemed to assume, including me, that having raised four baby boys we knew what we were doing. But Jennifer became a quick blessing to all our boys who soon learned the joys and challenges of having a baby sister. All her brothers would treat her well, but it was Jason who would be willing to spend the most time with her – he just seemed to enjoy little people more than his brothers. It was so different to have a little girl in our midst. Jennifer would prove to be a very caring person whose innocent joy of life has blessed us so wonderfully through the years.

So as life tends to do, it continued to move on. Our family was complete, and like many Canadians, we had truly very little to complain about. Life was good and we thanked the Lord daily for His blessings.

Blink and You'll Miss It

Somehow the lives of modern Canadians have arrived at a place of being far too busy. It always seems that there is not enough time in each day to complete everything. Our family was no different. Between the busy life of leading a church, music lessons, soccer games, and a seemingly inexhaustible list of other things, time raced past me like I was standing still. One day I turned around and our eldest, Jeff, caught my eye. Astonished, I realized that he resembled a man more than a boy. I barely had time to take a breath before Mark surged past me on his way to 6'2" tall. Before I knew it, Jason was looking down on me (I'm 5'8") from a similar lofty height, followed seconds later by Matthew.

In the ongoing hustle of life my guys had suddenly transformed into young men. It must have taken me at least two years to come to grips with this development – it really set me back. Thankfully I have enjoyed every stage of life with my children. It is true that the teen years are challenging. But even with the usual rebellion that marks the passage toward adulthood, it has been a blessing to be a dad. I don't think there has ever been a more important job or responsibility that I've had or ever will have. I'll admit there were times I wished I could turn the clock back. There are those moments where I'd like to redo the job of being dad a little better, but as St. Peter wrote, "Love covers a multitude of sins." And I love my children.

Challenges Unknown

Despite my lack of preparation for the maturing of our boys, life was going along fairly smoothly until '94. In the midst of grade ten Mark came down with strep throat. We thought nothing of it and the doctor prescribed the usual penicillin. After a couple of days there was no change. A subsequent visit saw Mark admitted to the hospital for dehydration. This was the beginning of a nightmare that would take us into one of those places no one wants to go.

In the hospital, Mark's condition worsened. He developed large ulcers (open sores that wouldn't heal – these were not canker sores) in his mouth and throat. The doctors bombarded him with several different antibiotics intravenously. For a time the situation seemed to settle down. Mark came home after a week but he was pale and wobbly. Roughly two weeks later these sores came back with a vengeance. Over the next month a number of doctors tried to discover what was wrong. These large, open sores would not go away and were excruciatingly painful. Mark's weight dipped close to one hundred pounds, and for a tall, already thin guy, the dramatic weight loss wasn't good.

One Friday morning I returned home from visiting a parishioner in the hospital. Diane told me that Mark could no longer swallow the "Boost" drinks that were his only source of sustenance. He was also having trouble breathing. At that point I had had enough. I immediately drove him to the Lethbridge Regional Hospital demanding that Mark be treated *now*.

The internist who had been working with him wanted to find out what was wrong before he treated him. At this point, even the doctor realized that something had to be done to treat the symptoms. They immediately put him on prednisone to shrink the sores. By noon the next day Mark was able to eat solid food for the first time in weeks, albeit painfully. This of course was not the solution to the problem. Indeed we would spend several months with countless doctors poking and prodding. One of the rheumatologists suggested this was an autoimmune system problem. Compared to the other physicians, he seemed garrulous. Basically they had no idea what the problem was. So Mark was put on a drug called immurin to suppress his immune system and kept on prednisone to control the sores. We were not happy with the lack of communication, nor the failure to find a cause. Under this regimen of drugs Mark somehow managed to function. He had little energy and his road to any kind of recovery would be long and painfully slow. I'm sure he would tell you that the side effects of the drugs were more distressing at times than the pain of the sores.

Through it all, I admired this young man who didn't complain or whine about his circumstances. And, though he missed six or seven weeks of school, with great determination (still hounded by pain and sickness) he caught up by the end of the school year and managed an 80 percent average. Through it all we sent up a barrage of prayers. I remember one particular day praying and crying all the way to Calgary, about a three-hour drive. I know that the Lord brings healing to people and I certainly wanted to see Mark healed. In this situation the instant healing I so desired did not happen.

Mark remained on the drugs for over four years, slowly weaning himself off them. The sores persisted after he stopped taking the medication but he refused to go back on the drugs. Today Mark is still medication free but he isn't back to 100 percent. He really can't participate in activities that call for much physical exertion. He tires easily and gets little sores in his throat. Sometimes he will go through a phase where getting to sleep is next to impossible. I continue to pray and believe that the Lord will complete this healing, and I hope it is soon.

Through five children this was our first experience with any serious health problems. The experience has taught me how draining it is to have someone you love come down with a long-term illness. I have always known it is more difficult to see someone you care about suffer, especially your own child, than it is to be ill yourself. Having spent time in children's intensive care units, I see that this reality is all too common for many people.

A Mission of a Different Kind

Jeff, our eldest son, graduated high school in the spring of 1996. He had planned to go on a short-term mission not long after, having found a group in the U.S. that did missions into Eastern Europe and South America. This particular organization worked through sports and that was a big draw for Jeff. They would gather young people and create several different sports teams. They then set up a tour playing other sports teams in whatever country they were visiting. Jeff had enjoyed playing soccer since he was seven years old. So this opportunity to play soccer in Venezuela, travel with forty or so teens, and share his faith, had great appeal for him.

We spent time that spring raising funds so he could go on his trip. At our annual church picnic I volunteered to sit in the dunk tank. Anyone could throw three balls for a dollar. We made a good bit of money that day and it took probably ten minutes before someone finally hit the bull's eye. Yes, the water was cold and I ended up taking several dunkings.

Jeff was to fly off for two weeks that July. When the time came, he was delayed one day by a hurricane in Florida, but he made it. He went without knowing anyone else on the team and I give him credit for that. It's not easy as a teenager to make trips by yourself. Upon his return we discovered that it was a good time. He had learned a lot about the country, lost a few soccer games, and made a few friends. Not long after his return, some substantial long distance phone bills began to crop up, and we realized that one of these friendships was significant. Her name was Angela and she hailed from Michigan. Jeff had always been a bit of a shy guy so this became, as far as we know, his first serious relationship.

This long distance romance began to bloom despite the obvious difficulties. So later the next spring, Jeff set out on a two-week journey to Michigan. That summer it was her turn to make the trek and we finally met this Angela who had grabbed our son's heart. She was a nice young girl who had grown up under some trying circumstances. The relationship plunged headlong forward and later that fall we were given word that Jeff was engaged.

Like any parents in that situation, we expressed a little concern over their ages. However, Di and I had been married when we were only twenty so we couldn't object too strenuously. In the summer of 1997 we all packed up and made the trip to Michigan for Jeff's wedding. It was a strange time and I guess I wasn't ready to see any of my children get married. All went well however, and we now had a new daughter. Jeff and Angie moved up to Calgary after the honeymoon to begin their new life together. We were thankful for this because visits to Michigan would have been few and far between. It didn't take much time for me to learn to bite my tongue and hold any advice unless it was asked for. A year later they prematurely blessed us with our first grandchild, Jessica. Life was changing way too fast for me. How could this all have happened so fast? Of course everything would soon pale in comparison to the events that were yet to come.

Black Wednesday

The day of April 28, 1999 was a black day for our family indeed. So much occurred on that day and so much was a blur. So in order for you to receive a greater picture of how that day impacted my family, a few of them have added their accounts of the day. Much of the information will be the same, some won't – but the point of view will change.

Dale

Life continued to stampede forward and brought more changes on what seemed a daily basis. Mark graduated high school in June of '97 and by the fall of '98 moved to Calgary to work for a while. Jeff and Angela were going through big adjustments being newly married and new parents as well. On the home front, Jason was working part time at the Mohawk service station where Mark had also worked. That fall he obtained that all-important driver's license. Matthew kept busy by trying to find new ways to ignore his schoolwork. I would say he was quite gifted at it, too. They were all growing so much faster than you can imagine, unless you have kids of your own.

Moving into 1999, we were finally learning to accept that we were growing older and our children were growing up. It was so good having Jennifer around. She was only seven and not ready to leave the nest just yet. Like most of us, I noticed that the older you get the faster life appears to fly by. The winters in southern Alberta began to feel long about the middle of January and I was glad to see spring come. Thankfully, it seemed to come a little faster than normal in this last year of the millennium.

As we burst into spring, Easter came and went in a flash and we were busier than ever. Before we knew it April 28 had come upon us. This date had been a special day for us since 1977 because it was the day Jeff had been born. April 28 was a Wednesday in 1999. The day began with the usual routine of showers, breakfast, and getting kids off to school. Diane and I had planned a quick trip into Lethbridge to hunt down a birthday present for Jeff. I remember the day well. It was overcast, one of those days that can't seem to make up its mind whether to be winter or spring.

In Lethbridge, we scrounged around and found a couple of things we thought Jeff would enjoy for his birthday. Then we grabbed a fast-food lunch and headed back home. We arrived about 1:10 that afternoon. Walking up to the front door of our house we could hear the phone ringing inside. I hurried with the key to catch the phone before it stopped ringing. It was the church line (it rings in our house as well as the church). I picked it up with the usual "Hello, St. Theodore's Anglican Church."

The response came back, "Is this Dale Lang?"

"Yes," I said.

The male voice on the other end continued immediately: "This is the hospital calling. Your son Jason is in the emergency unit and it's very serious. Please come to the hospital right now."

"What happened?"

He nervously responded, "I can't tell you over the phone. Please come immediately."

Waves of nausea swept through my stomach as I hung up the phone. Pale, I turned to Diane and shared with her what had been said. We headed out the door for the hospital blanketed by a cloud of confusion and fear. In the small town of Taber it is only a five-minute drive to the hospital. That short drive still seemed an eternity as we wondered together what could have gone wrong and how *serious* was serious? Jason had purchased a used car just two days earlier and I was fearful that he might have been involved in a car accident. I couldn't fathom anything else having gone wrong.

We pulled into the hospital parking lot as that low, grey sky started to release a few drops of rain. Rushing into the emergency unit of our hospital we were met at the door by the person who had called.

He greeted us with the words: "Jason has been *shot.*"

Those words just ripped through me, shredding everything in their path. So stunning were they that my mind immediately went into a state of denial. Thoughts began racing at warp speed. There has to be a mistake – this couldn't be happening to us! This couldn't happen to our son, here in Taber? Could it? I remember fumbling with my mouth to blurt out a question.

"Where was he?" I asked. I've had some time to reflect back on that day now. I think I asked that question because of an outdated thought that was floating somewhere in the back of my mind. The thought came from growing up in the Calgary area. To be shot there during my youth, you had to be in the wrong part of town or involved with the wrong kind of people.

The response came back: "Jason was shot at school." Those words had an even greater impact on us than the first pronouncement. It had only been eight days earlier that we had heard, and of course, seen the horrible tragedy at Columbine High School in Littleton, Colorado. Our family, like many others, had watched some of the news coverage of that event. I remember talking about it around the supper table. In hindsight, it strikes me that we had a fairly typical Canadian reaction. Even though this was obviously a terrible event, we did not really personalize it because it was in the United States. I think that often we Canadians have seen these American tragedies as just that – American. We seem to believe that such events don't cross the border, as if we are somehow immune, or perhaps slightly better than our neighbours to the south. On this day, that myth would be totally eradicated from my mind forever.

Now in shock, and obviously upset, Diane and I sat down in the waiting area of the emergency unit. We held hands and we prayed for Jason. A few minutes later someone came out of the room where they were working to save Jason's life. We immediately stood up as this person began walking toward us. I don't know if it was the look on their face but the thought that came to me at that moment was, "I don't want to hear this."

This person came over to us and very quietly said, "Jason didn't make it."

This moment for me remains impossible to describe verbally. Words often fail us at the deepest times of life and that is true here. I have never felt such emptiness in all my days. Some sixteen years earlier we had lost Diane's dad to cancer. While that was a painful time, in this moment the blackness was virtually unbearable. Blackness is really the only way I can even begin to describe it, but even that word falls infinitely short of an accurate expression. My life in that moment, which had been so blessed and so rich, now seemed totally empty of meaning and purpose. It is truly not possible nor is it fair to compare the pain people experience in different situations of loss. I had walked with two different families through the loss of children. My experience had told me there was something profoundly worse about losing a child. Now I was in the midst of every parent's worst nightmare. I wanted out. I wanted so desperately to change this thing. I wanted Jason to be alive. At that moment I would have gladly traded my life for his. I had lived forty-seven great years and he was only seventeen. There were so many adventures in life ahead of him. I so badly wanted him to have those adventures.

Those first few moments, knowing Jason's fate, seemed like I was stuck in an eternal moment of unbearable pain. I can't describe the shock of walking through an ordinary, average day, and then in an instant everything changes – drastically. It was like entering something totally unreal, like walking into another world. At first, I don't think I could comprehend what was happening to us. My mind wanted so desperately to deny this possibility. The really bad things always happen to someone else, somewhere else, don't they? I know it sounds naïve, but in our heart of hearts, most of us really believe that until we're forced out of it.

I remember sort of walking around for a few seconds, completely numb. I couldn't cry and I could hardly speak. Diane, as I recall, was in much the same state of mind. I paced back and forth. I held Diane. People, I am not even sure who, were talking to us. If there has ever been a moment in my life when I felt like dying, it was right then. A couple of minutes into this shock, Diane began to cry. At that point I still could not.

Someone asked if we wanted to go into the room where Jason's body was. I guess we said yes because shortly thereafter we entered that room. This was somehow necessary, but so tormenting and painful to do. I remember looking down at Jason. He just looked like he was asleep, almost. I guess they must have fixed things up a little before letting us in. Oh how I wanted him to wake up. I had just recently read a book that chronicled different people of the Christian faith. A man by the name of Smith Wigglesworth, who lived in the first half of the twentieth century, came to mind. In his ministry some thirteen people who had been clinically pronounced dead were brought back to life. I desperately wanted Jason to come back to life. As I looked down at him lying on that hospital table, the tears finally broke and poured out. Sobbing heavily I cried out to the Lord. I leaned over Jason's lifeless body and I prayed that Jesus would raise him from the dead.

Somehow, even as I prayed, I knew it wasn't going to happen. Diane would later tell me that in that moment she had total confidence that God could raise people from death. Yet she knew, too, that this was not going to happen for Jason. Predictably, people did not leave us alone with Jason for long. I remember telling him how much I loved him and how I was so sorry for what had happened to him. When parents lose children they most often feel a sense of guilt and responsibility. After all, parents are supposed to protect their children. This feeling, I have discovered, never leaves you. Once you are a parent you are a parent for life. No matter the age of your children, you feel a desire to help them and protect them.

The criminal nature of the situation necessitated the presence of an RCMP officer, so our few minutes with him were not alone. They had to watch over the situation because everything was evidence. When we came out of that room, my brain began functioning a bit more. I remember thinking about what had happened with a little more clarity. Who had shot Jason? For a few brief moments, anger came upon me very strongly. Jason was a quiet guy who did not hurt people. It was so wrong and so unjust that this likeable guy should be dead for no reason. It made me mad.

Thinking back, it surprises me how unfocused that emotion was. I never actually directed my anger at the boy who had killed Jason. I didn't even feel anger toward God. I was just mad that Jason was not alive. He should be alive and he should be able to live out his life. Thankfully, God intervened in my thoughts at this time. I began to think about how this country, full of blessing, freedom, and advantage, was so broken. There shouldn't be any reason for young people to be hurting and even killing each other. These thoughts that the Lord brought to me transformed my anger to sadness on the spot. No one had to say anything to me about the boy who shot Jason. I already knew he must be a troubled kid. So I became sad, and in this time of deep grief I never again returned to anger, even today.

By this time one of our parishioners had arrived. A lovely lady named Eva, whose eldest son was one of Jason's closest friends. Soon after her came Mike Rose. Mike had been doing youth work in our congregation for several years with his wife, Andrea. At that time, Mike worked in Lethbridge and yet he was the second person to make it to the hospital. The next several minutes would see the arrival of a number of people from our congregation. Members of New Life Church, a congregation we often worked with, arrived as well.

The next half-hour was a time for many tears and hugs. Jennifer was brought over to the hospital from her elementary school fairly quickly. However, it took longer for Matthew to arrive from the high school. It was the crime scene and for safety the kids had all been held in classrooms and the gym.

In the midst of this, with all the emotion and activity, we assumed that Matthew knew of Jason's death, but he did not. For about five minutes he was with us believing that Jason had only been injured. He had been told this at school, I guess for several reasons. In the end it was not helpful because finally something was said and he realized what had happened. We felt so bad for Matt as he had a sort of double shock. They must have assumed that it would be better for him to hear it from us, but the way he found out was not good. Over the next while we saw some thirty people gather with us at the hospital. Jason's two best friends came and there was continued shock and deep weeping.

It felt as though we were stuck in a whirlwind of circumstance and emotion. But at some point in all of this, I realized I had to phone Jeff, Mark, and other family. I will never forget how painful it was to share such horrid news over the phone. I could barely speak through my own weeping. It was almost as hard delivering the news as it had been receiving it.

Eventually the hospital staff moved our group into the boardroom. I can't overstate how important to us it was that friends came and were there to cry with us and love us. Agonized by those black, desolate moments, their presence made a huge difference. Amazingly, in that boardroom a sense of peace slowly descended and settled like dew. It wasn't that the pain was gone or even that the shock was gone. Looking back on it, I realize how powerfully the presence of God was there.

Tears continued to flow and there was some prayer, but not much was being said. When Matt had been brought over from the school a crisis counsellor had come along. This woman was in the boardroom with us. At a particular, and needed, moment of natural silence, this person felt the need to speak up.

She said, "Perhaps it would be a good time to talk about how we all felt when we heard the news?" The lady meant well, but I could not think of a more inappropriate thing for someone to say in that moment of silence. No one said a single word and the ensuing quiet was rather awkward. Everyone knew this question was more than unhelpful and I think the lack of response informed her of her error. I would realize in the days to come that this crisis response approach left much to be desired.

I knew it was inevitable but still wasn't sure if it would ever come. Then a time finally arrived when it seemed right to leave the hospital. Mike Rose insisted on driving our family home. I remember pulling out of the hospital parking lot as the late spring snow was falling all around us. It all seemed so very empty. There was little to say and much to feel. The days ahead would be filled with continuing pain, many tears and unexpected blessing.

Arriving back home the house seemed so very hollow. Jeff and Angela, as well as Mark, were on their way from Calgary. We were worried about their safe travel down to Taber. The last thing we needed was more bad news that day. Mike graciously stayed with us until the kids arrived. As you will read, Mike and Andrea's friendship and faith would be an invaluable blessing to us over the next few days.

The arrival of Jeff and Angela, and a little later Mark, would be the first of many tear-filled embraces in the entrance of our home. It defies description how the sense of loss and the empty feeling impacts you. How even months later your mind still hopes to convince you that there has been some kind of mistake – that this did not and could not happen to your son and family.

Before the family arrived from Calgary I felt the need to go over to the school and retrieve Jason's car. It was parked down the street from the now empty school, adorned with a thin layer of wet spring snow. The dim streetlight revealed the now deserted streets in front of the school. This whole setting seemed oddly surreal to me.

I climbed into Jason's Camaro and turned the key. Diane thought I should wait until the next day to get the car, but for some reason I couldn't do that. Maybe I felt a need to look after his car, make sure that it was okay. Maybe I thought that bringing his car home would somehow bring him home. I really don't know. At any rate, I think he would have wanted me to do that.

How appropriate it seemed to me that the night was dark and cold with wet snow gently falling. The weather fit my feelings and the unimaginable events that had come to our lives. Driving the car home that night, I could have driven out of town and down the highway, never to return. Running away would not ease the pain, let alone stop it. Still the urge was there and was somehow quite appealing.

Late in the evening an RCMP officer appeared at the door. He informed us that there would be a press conference in Taber the next day. He suggested that if we would produce a statement they would be happy to read it at the press conference. The hope was that this might help keep the media from bothering our family. This seemed like a reasonable idea to us, so we agreed to prepare a statement.

The shock and the horror of what happened still makes that day seem surrealistic to me. Perhaps there is still a hidden hope that I am just living through a very long nightmare – that I could wake up one day to life as it had been and should be, with all our children present and doing well.

Jeff

Hi, my name is Jeff. I am Jason's oldest brother. For what it's worth, I guess it's my turn to tell my account of this tragic yet amazing story. At the time of Jason's death, I was not living at home in Taber with my parents and family. I was newly married and living about two hours north in Calgary, Alberta, with my wife and young daughter, and my brother Mark. I didn't have the closest relationship with Jason at the time, but he was always the first to ask about my daughter when I talked to him and we were starting to build a good friendship rather than just being brothers because of an obligation. Enough of that though, let me get right to the story – the story through my eyes.

I was working in Calgary as a truck driver hauling propane around the city for refuelling. I remember it as being a cool and cloudy day. Coincidentally, it was also my twenty-second birthday. I received an unusual call over the truck radio that I was to return to the shop immediately. No explanation was given. By the time I pulled my truck into the shop yard I was more worried about losing my job than anything else. I still couldn't figure out any other reason for this situation. The branch manager told me that there had been a family emergency and I was to leave for home right away. I tried to press him for more details but he wouldn't tell me anything other than that my wife had phoned crying and I had to go. I can hardly remember what went through my mind as I raced through city traffic for the half-hour ride home. My first thoughts were of my daughter. Had something happened at home? Or maybe it was my grandfather who had been in and out of the hospital lately. To try and ease my mind I flicked on the radio. It wasn't long before I caught a news flash about a school shooting in Taber at my old high school. My mind raced around in circles. I had two brothers in that school still, Matt and Jason. One of them must have been hurt in this horrific event, but which one? At this point the thought of death never even crossed my mind. I completely avoided that scenario and assumed that one of them had been injured.

As I pulled up at home and ran to the door, Mark was already there with a look of bewilderment on his face. My wife fought back tears as she told me that Jason had been killed. I wouldn't believe it at first. "Are you sure he's not just hurt?" I asked more than once. After being assured without a doubt that Jason had been killed, my next thought turned to anger against the kid who had committed this terrible act. I wanted to know who he was so I could put the blame and anger onto someone. That feeling was replaced by concern for my parents when my dad called as we were on our way out the door.

He could barely say anything but my name, and my heart just went out to them. As we sped down the highway to Taber, a gloomy spring snow started to fall; it kind of fit the day for me.

When we got to my parent's house in Taber, we were greeted at the door by my mom and dad with deep sobs and hugs. I hadn't really ever seen my parents cry like this growing up and it really hit me. There were many people from the church and the community already there to support us. At first I was frustrated at having all these people around, but later I realized how valuable it was. The amazing thing about it was that my parents, as deeply grieving as they were, seemed to be doing more comforting of people than they were being comforted by people. The next morning I awoke to the sound of my mother sobbing deeply upstairs. It was deeper than I've ever heard anyone sob before. I wanted to go and comfort her but somehow I knew that she might need this alone time, away from everybody else. It still boggles my mind when I think about what happened and how God blessed our family in spite of it. It's almost impossible to describe all the feelings I was overwhelmed with that day. But, in the end, God's grace touched our family in a very tangible way and without that, I don't think I would have made it through.

Mark

It was the beginning of a long, transitional season in my life. It started with a move from the small town of Taber to Calgary. The move had broken my stale routine and created a fresh feeling I hadn't experienced in years. Like a crisp spring morning there was an invigorating haze settling over my new life in the big city. Being debilitated by an immune system *malfunction* – so the doctors called it, as if I was a car or something – throughout my high school years, I had spent an acrimonious period of time locked away in small rooms, the foremost being my bedroom, and the various hospital rooms I loathed. The move, however, had provided a long-awaited distraction from my still-ailing body and a necessary change of scenery. It wasn't a particularly hard decision to leave Taber, really. I had never overly enjoyed life there. The incredible contrast of Pittsburgh to this small prairie town had never digested well in my system. To this day, my time spent in Pittsburgh still registers as some of the most blessed days I've ever spent on this earth. Childhood memories are often distorted, but God's hand was on our entire family in a different way in Pittsburgh. Not that we weren't blessed in Taber, it was just different and I guess I never liked the switch.

After arriving in Calgary, I spent only one day job searching (which consisted of randomly dropping off a handful of résumés in Calgary's Southeast). I was promptly offered two jobs and began to work in a flooring warehouse. Before long I had settled into my new city and was enjoying life.

Time seemed to slip between my fingers and before I could breathe, Christmas had arrived. I had not seen my parents or younger siblings since the beginning of October, so it was nice to see them pull into my grandparents' driveway that afternoon. Our Christmas family gatherings were uneventful but good that year. Before I knew it, the family had returned home leaving my older brother's family and myself behind in Calgary. This was the last I saw of Jason.

Time has not been very effective at eroding my memories of April 28, 1999. I was still in transition, an awkward time in my life. I had just made the natural progression from the flooring warehouse to the installing end of the business. I had no intention of making a career out of it and, realistically, my damaged body wouldn't have fared well very long in that job. Visions of grandeur waltzed around my brain with thoughts of furthering my education as their partner. I really had no idea what God's call was on my life or where He fit in. Thankfully at least one of us could see straight. I was a confused nineteen year old who knew things had to change, but I wasn't sure what to change. Anyway, I had moved in with my older brother, his wife, and my beautiful niece several months earlier. We lived in a tiny condominium in Southwest Calgary. My room seemed the size of a toy chest, but it was home.

That morning I was rather sluggish and not really awake. It's funny though, the smallest things from that day are etched in my memory. I can remember stepping outside onto our ridiculously scant piece of dead grass called a yard. It was so peaceful, even for Calgary. The sky was overcast and the air was cool but it had no bite. Fluffy rolling cumulus clouds floated overhead, gently caressing the sky. The sun had just managed to find a weakness in the wall of clouds. Warm honey-like fingers of light grazed across my face welcoming me to the day. A robin was perched on the second lowest branch of a tree in the courtyard and rhythmically chirped his tune. It was so surreal and it seems overdone, but I remember it so clearly. The most minor details just haven't left my mind.

The smell of morning dew was rising off the grass as I tromped toward my car. Fortunately, I was working on a job only a short drive away and traffic wasn't a problem. My boss and I were installing new linoleum in a kitchen and dining room that day. I can still remember the faces of the couple who lived in that house. This was one thing I had already begun to like about my new job. We got to work in a different environment each day, eliminating some of the monotony I'd experienced at the warehouse. By noon we were ready to install the new floor, so we decided to grab a bite to eat before finishing the job. After driving my boss across town to the Northeast, so he could run an errand, we stopped at a burger joint not far from the job and ate lunch.

After finishing our meal, we headed back to the house and began making our cuts on the piece of linoleum. We were literally right in the middle of laying it when my boss' cell phone rang. After a short conversation, which I ignored, he hung up and simply said, "You have to go home now."

You must understand that this particular job required two people. The two rooms were connected via an open doorway, and there were several nooks and crannies along with a closet that had to be dealt with. We planned on using only one piece of linoleum for both rooms, increasing the difficulty. It wasn't rocket science but it definitely required both of us. This in mind, I responded to the little information I had by saying, "What about the job?"

"Don't worry about it, you have to go home now! There's a problem," he replied.

"OK, but I'll try to get back as quick as I can to help you finish." That was the extent of the conversation. Oddly, I was not that worried about this turn of events as I left the house that day.

As I strolled toward my car the weather was getting nastier. My mind was busy analyzing different scenarios urgent enough to pull me from work. My first thought was that maybe my older brother had been in an accident – he drove a large propane truck at the time. This thought scared me, but somehow I knew Jeff was fine. Drifting, my thoughts moved to my baby niece. Maybe she had become ill and needed a ride to the doctor. After all, it was difficult to find Jeff during the day and I was close by. To be honest, neither of these thoughts really held any weight with me. I figured that it was probably something that had been overexagerrated and no big deal. I couldn't have been more wrong if I'd tried.

I must emphasize that I really didn't think anything major was wrong. So as I got in my car to drive home, I nonchalantly turned on the radio. The first thing I heard was the disc jockey saying, "After this break we'll have more information on the incident at W.R. Myers High School in Taber."

I don't know on which Caribbean island my brain was vacationing that day, but I still didn't clue in at this point. My only thought was, "Huh, that's kind of funny, I went to W.R. Myers High School." When the DJ came back on, I was not far from home and what I was about to hear was not good. He said that there had been a shooting at the high school. Two students had been shot, one was dead and one was in serious condition. At this point my brain re-entered the atmosphere and everything suddenly and terribly made sense. My mind went from 0 to 60 in about a second. My first thought was that I had two brothers in Myers, Jason and Matthew. Jason was in Grade 11 at the time and Matt was in his first year of high school in Grade 9.

Looking back, I recognize the reason I was so nonchalant. I honestly didn't believe anything could happen to Jeff or Jessie. But it was also more than that – somehow I knew that they were fine. Likewise as I thought about Matthew, I was at peace. I knew he was fine. Unfortunately that left Jason, and suddenly it hit me like a ton of bricks. Without a doubt, before I had talked to anyone in my family, I knew Jason was no longer with us. I can't describe or explain these feelings very well, but I can remember it clearly. There was no question in my mind. I was so convinced that I didn't even plead with God (Don't let it be one of my brothers, Lord!) because I knew it was Jason.

As this bombshell reverberated through my body, the grace of God pulled me from my haze. I realized that I was racing down Richmond Road forty kilometres an hour over the limit. The engine of my car whined loudly because I hadn't even remembered to switch gears.

Within minutes I arrived home and parked the car. A breeze had picked up in the afternoon and swept by me as I walked toward our condominium. Approaching the yard, I could see my sister-in-law waiting at the door. She stepped outside as I entered the yard, a deep sadness in her eyes. Honestly I really didn't pay attention to what she was saying – I already knew. Finishing, she gave me a hug and retreated back inside.

I'm really at a loss for words to describe my emotional state at this point. I could say that I felt an intense sorrow, but actually I don't think I really felt it because everything was buried deep beneath an avalanche of shock. From this shock ensued numbness which seemed to permeate my entire body. It all just melted into a surreal feeling, very much like a dream. Everything kind of froze at that moment for me. I don't recall any thoughts going through my head at all. I don't know how long I sat there engulfed by that lonely silence, but before I knew it, Jeff was coming up the path toward the house. He had a puzzled look on his face. As he entered the yard, I relayed the terrible news. I think it was harder to tell Jeff the news than it had been to find out myself. A hug ensued and I think he was probably as numb as I was.

I can remember entering the condo and heading up to my room. I think that was the longest set of stairs I've ever climbed. Entering my room, I closed the door and turned on the CD player. Tears were rolling down my face and yet I still wasn't feeling anything. I lay on my bed in complete disarray emotionally and intellectually. It's really an odd thing to be crying and feel no emotional accompaniment to the tears.

Shortly thereafter I heard a knock at my door. It was my sister-in-law wanting to know if I was all right. I guess she was reacting the only way she knew how, but all I wanted was to be left alone. Thankfully she took my word at face value and left. I don't know how well I would have reacted to pestering.

Sometime later, I heard the phone ring downstairs. Knowing it was probably Mom or Dad, I went down to the living room to investigate. By this time one of my uncles had stopped by the house to see us. Jeff answered the phone and it was Dad on the other end. Tears cascaded down Jeff's face as he listened. Neither of them could get through an entire sentence without being overwhelmed by emotion. I will never forget that conversation as long as I live. It's times like that when the unseen depth of the bonds between us manifest and become plainly visible.

Before long, we all headed upstairs to begin packing in preparation for the trip home. The numbness had really settled on me, but it was weird because there would be sudden outbursts of emotion (like when Dad called) and then nothing again. Most of all I just wanted to be left alone. So when we were ready to leave, I informed Jeff I would be taking my own car instead of travelling with them. They didn't like the idea of me being alone, but I insisted. I took my time driving home that day. Jeff and Angela arrived there long before I did. I needed the time by myself to cry, to talk to the Lord, to think, to try and grasp what had actually happened.

I pulled up to the house still in a daze and more numb than ever. I was so out of it, I failed to notice all the vehicles around. Mom and Dad greeted me at the door and we all broke down together, weeping deeply. Inside, the house was swelled with fifteen or twenty people, all wonderful friends or relatives who had come to console the family.

It really was amazing the support we received. I can remember two of my friends, Danny and Darren, were waiting for me. I am thankful for my friends and everybody who was there. It was wonderful support for my parents and siblings. But the truth is that coming home, still in shock and wanting to be alone, having the house full like that really sucked. I don't mean to sound ungrateful or mean, but that is really how I remember it – it sucked. I couldn't get away and everywhere I turned someone else (some of whom I didn't know) was asking me how I was doing. After years of being sick and having people constantly ask that question, it was really the last thing I wanted to hear. I just wanted to be left alone but there was nowhere to hide, the house was so packed. Eventually people began to leave and go home. Those of us left all hunkered down and got ready for a sleepless night, the first of several.

Jennifer

The day my brother was shot I was in Grade One. It was right after bathroom break and we just got settled into class. I was learning, when all of a sudden I heard lots of ambulances. I never liked the sound of an ambulance but this one was different, it scared me a lot more. Then the principal said on the intercom, "All staff members to the office for a meeting." He never does that in the middle of class.

Then we had to go into the Grade 2 room to sing songs. Then the principal came in and said, "Jennifer is wanted at the door." It was my best friend's mom. We went into a white car and drove to the hospital. My dad was trying to make me laugh when I went in, but I didn't. Then we went into the waiting room and everybody was crying so I started crying even more. Then my mom said to me "Jason got shot with a gun at his school."

I got really scared and said, "Mommy, please don't cry."

She looked at me and said, "I'm sad, and mommies and daddies can cry, too."

So we were in the waiting room and there was a cloth with blood on it. My mom and dad asked me if I wanted to go see him. I said no. They tried to explain to me that it looked like he was sleeping but I still said no. When they went in to see him, I was sitting in the chair my mom had been sitting in, shivering. When they came back, my mom took me home. Then my dad came home, too. One of my mom's and dad's best friends was there, asking and telling us if we needed anything just holler.

My mom and I were sitting on the couch talking about memories of Jason. My dad made phone calls to other family members to tell them the bad news. That whole month or more we had people bringing flowers, presents, and cards to us. We had loads of mail and we still do, but not as much. The funeral was very sad and all I can remember is my brother crying. But now I forgive the boy who shot Jason.

Diane

Jason's "Graduation" Day

The morning of April 28, 1999, was typical of many in our household. It was the usual struggle getting Matthew and Jennifer up, fed, and on their way to school. My husband, Dale, and I then took care of a few errands before we headed into Lethbridge. It happened to be Jeff's twenty-second birthday, which had snuck up on us ever so quietly. We were looking forward to seeing Jeff, Angela, and our precious granddaughter, Jessica, on the weekend for some birthday celebrations.

Dale had also taken Jason, our third son, for a driving lesson that morning before school. Jason had wanted to get some practice time in his newly acquired Camaro. It was very unusual for Jason to be out of bed so early on a school morning. He didn't know how to drive a manual transmission very well yet, and that was motivation enough to get him up, I guess. Jason and Dale had a great half-hour together before we all went our separate ways. I remember saying to him as I went out the door, "Have a good day, Jason. We'll see you after school." Little did I know that these words would be my last communication with him.

Things had gone fairly smoothly up until this point in my life. I felt blessed, secure, and comfortable with the way things were. Adding to this feeling was the excitement of several things going on around us. There was a new sense of the Holy Spirit moving in our congregation and several of our church members were hungry for more of God. It had been at our church conference a month prior where things had turned around. We saw God move in a mighty way through the guest speaker who had come. After going through a long time of drought, our hearts were set back on fire during this time. Things were good and we were looking forward to the future.

In retrospect, I am in awe of how God prepared the people of our church for what was to come. If God had not stirred our church, and if we hadn't been renewed, things might have been very different. Dale and I personally would not have had the ability to walk through the coming devastation. We were so tired and worn out before that church conference. Likewise, that touch from God changed the congregation significantly. We may not have had the same kind of support from them without that conference.

Anyway, we spent the morning in Lethbridge shopping and had lunch before heading back to Taber. I remember being very tired and a little down as we drove home. The day was grey and dull – it couldn't make up its mind whether to rain or snow. Arriving home, we were greeted by the telephone as soon as we walked in.

I knew that something was wrong immediately when Dale answered it. After hanging up, he hurriedly explained to me that Jason was in the hospital and we needed to get over there right away. Our minds were spinning with all of the possible things that could have gone wrong. They hadn't given us any details over the phone and we had no idea what was going on. Before heading out the door, we took a brief moment to pray. We asked for God's wisdom and strength because we had no idea what we would be facing. This short but heartfelt cry to Jesus was probably the most important thing that we did during this time. We were about to find out that when the "rubber meets the road" and your faith is put to the test, God is faithful and swift to answer the cries of His children.

Finally reaching the hospital, we ran into the emergency waiting room. I was amazed to see that so many people were gathered there. We still had no idea what was going on. It felt to me as if we had stepped into the middle of a nightmare in which we were the focus of everyone's attention, but were totally ignorant as to why.

As I looked around trying to decide what to do, the clusters of people began to part. Through this passage, a man walked toward us and introduced himself as the chaplain from the hospital in Lethbridge. I noticed another family was off to my right surrounded by a group of people. They were all crying softly and I remember thinking that I should go over and offer some sort of comfort. But at that moment the chaplain began to speak. He gently told us that Jason had been shot and that he was in critical condition. He said that the doctors were working on him.

I was totally stunned and there was no way to process the information. It just didn't make any sense at all. The idea that my son could have been shot was something that would never have crossed my mind. After all, this was Taber, a rural town with a population of just over 7,000 people. I looked at Dale's face and the tears that were starting to flow. I began to realize that this was not a dream, it was real, and I didn't know what to do. The only thing I could think of was that we needed to pray. This was something that was out of our control. I have no idea what people were thinking during this time. But everyone present felt our cries to Jesus and they quietly and reverently allowed us to intercede for them and us.

After a short period of time the chaplain, who had quietly gone back to the trauma room, reappeared. He carried the heart-wrenching news that our precious Jason was gone! The doctors had tried their best to save him but there was nothing else they could do. I hadn't realized that he was close to death. There hadn't been time to get details and I couldn't believe what I was hearing. I felt profoundly alone in the room and somehow detached from my body. I heard myself crying and I felt Dale take my hand. He pulled me toward him and we clung to each other, weeping bitterly. It was the worst moment I have ever experienced in my whole life! Others were crying around us but no one seemed to know what to say. There was no way to alleviate our grief. The chaplain invited us to come and spend time with Jason. This seemed right and necessary so we followed him into the trauma room, still in shock.

It came as a surprise to me to see my son lying on the table, looking as if he were asleep. Everything seemed so unreal at the time. I had an intense desire to tell him that it was time to wake up, get off the bed, and come home. He didn't look dead to me at all. He looked like he was sleeping and I wanted him to wake up. I stood for a while, not knowing if I should go closer to him. I felt as if I was intruding where I didn't belong.

The nurse said that we could touch him and hold his hands. Dale moved to the far side of the bed and began to stroke Jason's hair. He wept and prayed over him quietly. I felt as if he were praying for him the way Elisha prayed over the widow's son, "eyes to eyes, nose to nose, mouth to mouth." I was hoping that God, in His mercy, would raise Jason from the dead as he had done for that boy. In that moment I was given an incredible gift of faith to believe that God could actually raise my son from the dead! Even though I believed this was possible in that moment, I came to realize that it was not going to happen. I realized God was doing something much more incredible and all encompassing than any of us could imagine.

In the midst of the pain and sorrow during this time, I cried out to Jesus for my son, my family, and our community. I sensed an awesome peace in that room and I knew that I was not alone. I felt I had no choice but to totally trust God. I knew He would get us through whatever lay ahead. One of the hardest things that I have ever done was to leave my son in that hospital room. It was so hard to step out into the world, totally putting my faith on the line and surrendering all to Jesus. God's amazing love and grace have poured into my life as a result of that step. I can and will praise God and give thanks even in the death of my son, Jason, because of this. I am a different person today than I was on April 28, 1999. I have learned that God does keep His promises. I have also learned that if you let Him, He will take the tragic events of your life and pick up the pieces. He will fashion them into something that will be a blessing to you and to others and will bring honour to His name!

Caught in the Wake

Thursday, April 29

As the dead of night settled on our house that evening, no one was looking forward to bed. I have experienced sleepless nights before, like anyone else. But they all pale immensely when compared to that night of April 28. The clock agonizingly marked the slow march of seconds as they sauntered by, taunting my tired body. It was the longest night of my life.

I got up early the next morning – there was no reason to keep lying in bed awake. I went down to the computer in my study and began to formulate a statement for the press. I could hear the family stirring as I worked. Finishing, I took the statement to them. Everyone thought it was reasonable and so we agreed to use it. It was quiet that morning. There seemed little that could be said.

Somewhere around 9 a.m. an RCMP officer rang our doorbell. He came in and I handed him the statement for the 10 a.m. press conference. He left and I thought to myself, "Well, that is taken care of.

Hopefully the media won't bother us." Things were still quiet, as most of us seemed lost in our own thoughts when the doorbell rang again. I opened the door and there stood the RCMP officer. Their legal council had advised them not to read our statement. He suggested that if we wanted the statement to be released, a member of the family could read it. As a family, we were unsure of what to do. At first I didn't really want to speak to anyone. But as 9:30 a.m. approached, the thought of possibly keeping the press away kept nudging me. Finally I decided to go down to Taber's civic centre and read the statement.

As I got ready to head to the press conference, Jeff volunteered to come with me. I was certainly in need of the support and greatly appreciated it. We then made the short drive over to the centre. We entered a large room with one table in the middle of it. There were over 200 media people milling around. Feeling a little intimidated, I was led to the table and sat down beside the principal of W.R. Myers. Just a few feet away were the press, a virtual bee's nest of people, cameras, and microphones.

As the press conference got underway, the police were the first to speak. Before I knew it they were done, and it was my turn. I couldn't wait to get it over with, but at the same time I wasn't sure I was going to get through it. I just felt like bursting into tears, but by the grace of God I managed to speak clearly.

The Press Release

"The Lang family could never find the words to express the pain of the senseless loss of our son, Jason. He was a very fine young man, who loved life, played soccer, hockey, and golf, and enjoyed time with his friends. He loved little children, especially his seven-year-old sister whom he played with frequently. Most important, however, was his love for Jesus. It is that reality which gives us some peace in this time of chaos – knowing he is in that place Jesus called Paradise.

"Jason, just three days ago, got the car of his dreams and on April 28, his eldest brother's birthday, his incredible life came to an untimely end. We grieve for our son, for this community, and for the sad state of a fourteen-year-old boy who could come to such a place as randomly taking another person's life for no reason. May God have mercy on this broken society and all the hurting people."

The entire room was silent as I gave my statement. With the exception of the odd click of a camera, or buzz from the broadcasting equipment, you probably could have heard a pin drop. And, not only did God's grace allow me to read it clearly, but His wisdom and hand also must have been upon that statement. It would ring throughout the streets and halls of the nation for the next several days. Personally, I was still absorbed by shock and everything seemed so bizarre. I was just glad to have spoken coherently as I relayed it.

After what seemed an eternity, the press conference was over. I was glad to be able to leave that room behind. Things didn't get easier, though, as Jeff and I headed for the door. It seemed a herd of cameramen was walking in front of us taking video and stills. I can remember thinking how humorous it would have been if one of them had backed over a small cliff or something (not that I wished them any harm, but they were quite intimidating). Then again, maybe it wasn't so much the humour of the thought that appealed to me. Maybe I was just looking for anything to pull the attention away from Jeff and I. When the average person is faced with extreme (media) attention they often don't know how to react. But when you're still in a state of shock after having lost one of your sons, the last thing you need is to be hounded by a ravenous media, and hot on the heels of Columbine, it was a feeding frenzy.

Finally, after maneuvering through the media, we reached the van and made our getaway. As we returned home, I remember thinking that the media would leave us alone now that the press conference was over. Looking back, I should have known it wasn't going to be that easy.

The house was still quiet and peaceful when we returned. It was in these quiet times that God's presence in this terrible situation was so evident. Amidst our pain and anguish the Lord was there, holding us up. It was in the still of the morning when this was unmistakably clear to me. The Lord had walked each step with us, but it wasn't until that morning I realized how far He'd already carried us through. It would have been nice to sit and bask in the Lord for the rest of the day, even though I knew that was not going to happen. The shrill ring of our phone fractured the tranquil silence and brought my train of thought to a halt.

The voice on the other end was familiar, yet somehow I couldn't place it in my mind. It turned out to be Mike Paciello, an old friend and classmate from seminary whom I hadn't seen in several years. When a class of university students graduates there is always the inevitable parting of ways as each individual heads down the road of his career. The pastoral field is definitely no exception. Like buckshot from a shotgun, as soon as we were released, we spread out over North America permeating most corners and crevices of our cities and towns. Mike Paciello had been called to minister in the New York area.

I immediately wondered why Mike was calling. I couldn't imagine him knowing about Jason that quickly, but he was already passing along his sympathy and support. As the conversation progressed, he informed me that he had been driving in his car that morning (early afternoon in New York) and had heard the press conference live from our civic centre. He recognized my voice and upon hearing what had happened, he called. As silly as it sounds, I was a bit shocked and astounded that they could broadcast live from our little civic centre in the middle of nowhere. It was at this point that I actually began to realize how much attention was being paid to Jason's death.

Mike Paciello's call wasn't the last by any means. An unrelenting barrage of phone calls descended on our quiet house. The phone was literally ringing every five minutes or less. This phone blitz would eventually slow but it nevertheless continued for months and months afterward. Alongside the phone calls was the doorbell. It was almost as if someone had turned on a faucet, as a steady flow of people began to pour into our home. Many of them we didn't know very well, but it was good to talk to every last one.

Along with people from our church, friends and relatives, many of the townspeople stopped by to offer their condolences. This continued throughout the entire day, steadily filling our home with love and support. Many who came to the house that day brought food, flowers, and gifts. Others who couldn't make the visit in person sent gifts as well. It was a wonderful outpouring of support. I don't think anyone in our family ate much of anything – the stress of the situation had completely killed my appetite. Still, the wonderful support we received will never be forgotten. God truly has blessed us with extraordinary family and friends.

That same wonderful support was also exhausting in many ways. As the doorbell continued to ring, Diane and I continued to answer it. Each time somebody new came in, we greeted them and cried together. We couldn't help it. With each new face, the emotion came flooding to the surface with hurricane-like power. It was a weird place to be suspended. A constantly churning sea of emotion battered the inside of my soul, waiting for an opportunity to escape. Just when I had managed to get the surface stilled and peaceful, another wave of emotion would rise out of nowhere.

Among the many who entered our house that day, my own parents were a very welcome sight. They had travelled from their farm in Calgary, arriving in the early afternoon. The house was still buzzing with people, so Di and I took them into my study to have some time alone. My dad was never an outwardly emotional person. I can remember as a child how he always kept up a strong exterior, like the man of the house was expected to do. I remember watching him take a phone call from Winnipeg when I was a small boy. My dad's family was mostly situated in Winnipeg at that time. This particular phone call was not a happy one. He was given the news that his mother had passed away. I could see the pain and deep-rooted sorrow in his eyes but I don't remember any tears. In fact, I don't recall ever seeing Dad cry as I grew up. Now an elderly man, with the weight of time resting on his shoulders, he sobbed deeply and uncontrollably. I must admit this took me a moment to process. Even amidst the sea of tears and emotion we had been drenched in and surrounded by, I was still taken aback by my father's tears. The sheer nakedness with which his battered soul wept touched my heart and broke down any defences I had feebly been trying to build up. We all wept with our souls exposed and bare, leaning on one another for warmth and comfort.

My parents had always provided an abundance of love for my sister and I as we grew up. They had supported us both through many decisions they didn't agree with, and especially during the toughest times of our lives. When each grandchild had been welcomed into the world, this love had been easily reproduced. They had never shown any significant favouritism and loved each unique grandchild as their own.

Jason had just begun to grow into a quiet young man in recent years. They had relished his company a great deal as he matured. Dad had graciously given his old 1980 Chevy pickup to Jason for his first vehicle. Looking back, I now realize what a significant gift this truck was. It symbolized the unwavering powerful bond that had always been present between grandfather and grandson. Nurtured and grown between the two of them, this bond existed with all the grandchildren. Likewise, Jason, as he grew into that young man, had enjoyed visiting his grandparents and helping with maintenance around the acreage. All of our boys had spent time there doing work for their grandparents. You could find them painting, cutting grass, or just doing odd jobs around the homestead, and they all had enjoyed the time with Granny and Granddad. Jason, in particular, liked to drive the garden tractor, cutting the grass in the pasture.

I can't imagine what it must have been like for them to lose a loved grandchild. It is unnatural to see one of your children die before you do. You can never prepare for it and you never expect to see it. This is partly what makes it so unreal. You automatically assume you will not have to attend one of your own children's funerals – it's just not rational. Parlay this feeling into being a grandparent and I can only wildly grasp at what it might be like to lose a loved grandchild. It must be equally painful and even more surrealistic in nature than losing a child. Mom and Dad both wept hard that day and, like the rest of us, would go through many more times of tears in the days, months, and years ahead.

That day turned out to be one of the longest, most painful, and bizarre days I have or probably ever will experience. Thinking back, it was a very strange scene that day at the Lang house. People perpetually coming and going, the two phones ringing within several minutes of being hung up. It still amazes me when I think about some of the different calls we received. People from one end of the country to the other were calling the house. All kinds of people we had never met, but many broken and hurting people who themselves had been through much. It was a privilege to be able to share some of God's peace with them as many wondered how we were able to forgive. This theme of forgiveness was paramount and would eventually fuel a lot of interest in our situation and us.

Friday, April 30

After the events of Wednesday and Thursday, I was physically and mentally exhausted. Many people and much pain were the norm and it had been the most grueling twenty-four hours of my life. I just wanted to retreat to my bed and get lost in a peaceful slumber. I longed to escape from my own mind. It had not stopped churning since I had first taken that dreadful call from the hospital. You run almost every scenario possible through your mind after an event of such significant consequence. If only you'd kept him home from school, whatever the reason. If only you'd spent more time with him. Not that we hadn't spent plenty of time with him, but you grasp at any wild straw you can. Sleep, I had hoped, would silence my inner turmoil and allow for some semblance of peace. My bed had never looked so inviting and it wasn't long before I drifted off. I credit this sleep to sheer exhaustion because my mind still raced as I lay down. But thankfully I was able to find some elusive rest that night. I think I could have stayed in my bed forever, if that were possible.

As Friday dawned on the horizon there was no real hope of any serenity. I would have settled for just the eye of the storm, but that didn't materialize either. It would, however, turn out to be another extraordinary day filled with many decisions.

Friday was also a day of revelation for me in many ways. The attention this incident was beginning to command took me off guard. It was under the hot, stinging beams of the spotlight that the first revelation of the day hit me. *This was not only a significant incident for our family but it was turning into a significant incident for the country.* Over the next few days we would see an ever-increasing escalation of attention.

The onslaught of e-mails that flooded my account were the first indication of the impact this calamity was having. The ripples sent out from our situation were extending across the country with incredible speed. On the day of the shooting, Wednesday, a handful of e-mails had arrived. But, by Thursday and Friday hundreds upon hundreds of e-mails had washed in. Along with these e-mails there were also several Internet sites set up where people could post messages. They were all filled with letters of sympathy and encouragement.

All the e-mails that came over that period stayed on my computer for several years after. For whatever reason, I just never could delete them. I guess they were like a piece of family history. They brought back a kaleidoscope of vivid, painful, and happy memories all at the same time. Eventually I printed many of those messages and I keep them in my office. It's very interesting when I look back on them now. I can literally see how the flow of incoming e-mails just mushroomed as the days went by. It really was incredible how the word spread and how God began touching people.

We literally got e-mails from across the country, and it didn't stop there. People from all over the United States, Japan, and Germany sent their prayers and comfort. All over England they were praying, too. One of our church members happened to be in Britain at that time and heard about it there. We also received mail from Chile, South Africa, and from some missionary friends who were based in Uganda. As well, we were informed that seventy-five churches in Russia were sending up prayers for us. The support was remarkably coming in from around the globe. I still can't really believe that the long finger of our tragedy gripped so many people and touched so many nations.

At this point, I would like to share with you two excerpts from e-mails I received. The first was written by one of my personal mentors and a dear friend. I feel it's significant because it's a great example of the e-mails we were receiving. Also, whenever I look at it, I realize how precisely God answered the prayer in it. The second is a series of excerpts from an e-mail that Jim Berkley sent out (I'll explain about him later in the chapter). It gives further illumination to how much attention our situation was receiving. My hope is that it will help you understand just a little bit better what it was like to be in my shoes during those days. Here is the first excerpt:

> *Dear Dale, Diane and your loving children, we can't pretend to offer words that will take away the pain of your diabolical loss. Having commended Jason into the arms of the Lord, we pray that the Lord will rescue something good out of all this sorrow and give you a strength and peace more powerful than you have ever known.*

Every word of that prayer was answered infinitely and the Lord continues to answer it to this day. Here is the second set of excerpts:

> *Arriving at 10 a.m. this morning at the Calgary airport, I saw Pastor Lang's face and testimony all over the front page of every newspaper in Canada! I picked up a rental car to drive the three hours southeast to Taber. The radio talk shows were all filled with heart-searching discussions about this whole thing. Everywhere I went, I asked people what they thought of what has happened in Taber. They all, without exception, stopped what they were doing, many with tears in their eyes, said the same thing: "We don't know why this happened and we don't know what to do."*

Pastor Dale was on CBC [a Canadian TV Network] *yesterday morning to issue his statement....The nation's flags are all at half mast. The CBC has asked Pastor Lang to "come back on TV and just tell us* [Canada] *what we should do now!"....*

Monday, Pastor Dale will speak to the entire student body and to the nation as well at the memorial service!

We have heard that Mrs. Chrétien, the Prime Minister's wife, and the Premier of Alberta are making plans to attend the memorial service.

A TV station in British Columbia cancelled a violent program announcing to the viewers that they were doing this in honour of Jason....

God is so good and faithful beyond my comprehension. People were praying around the globe specifically for my family. That still just blows my mind and my God box whenever I think about it. I hope these excerpts helped illustrate the fury of attention toward the whole situation. And, if you were wondering, many of the incidents in Jim's e-mail will be explained later.

It wasn't just the e-mails that were rolling into the house. As I said previously, we received a myriad of phone calls. There are several that still stand out in my memory. It was early that Friday morning and the phone was incessantly ringing. I remember Diane taking a phone call from a lady in British Columbia. This particular lady, like many, had been especially touched and moved by Jason's death. This lady described how she had been unable to stop looking at Jason's picture in the paper. Somehow she sensed an incredible peace in the whole thing and couldn't figure out why. She then asked Diane if "he [Jason] was the one who was going to save us?" Diane responded by politely explaining that the peace she sensed was the peace of Jesus Christ. Diane then shared about how Jesus saved us and why we responded the way we did to our son's murder.

Another phone call Diane took was from a young man in nearby Lethbridge. In great detail he explained how he'd lived his entire life an atheist. Witnessing the response from our family had so impacted him that he had gone and talked with a local pastor. He just wanted us to know the major impression our incident was having on some people. Calls like these confirmed to me how many people there are in deep need and desperately searching for answers. These calls were also an incredible source of reassurance to us. God was creating some good out of our tragedy and the calls were tangible evidence of that. And, just like the e-mails, we were receiving calls of encouragement and prayer from around the world. I can't thank everyone enough for their support. In fact, I wouldn't even know where to begin.

The amazing attention being paid to us was also very evident through the media itself. I couldn't have been more wrong when I thought the media would leave us alone after our initial statement. And it wasn't long after the statement that I had sensed God was going to use our tragedy to reach a lot of people. The e-mails and phone calls had heightened this sense, but I think this feeling was really confirmed around mid-afternoon Friday. This confirmation came in the form of a phone conversation with a CBC (Canadian Broadcasting Corporation) employee.

It went something like this:

Reverend Lang, our director for the six o'clock television news would like to invite you to speak on today's news telecast if you feel up to it. He said we will give three minutes of time and you can say anything you want to.

My jaw hung limp as I listened to this proposal. The media in Canada was not exactly known for being pro-Christian. The CBC, in particular, had developed a reputation for being virtually the opposite. In my view, they tended to espouse anti-Christian out-looks. I'm sure they are usually very careful not to posture them-selves into such a vulnerable place. There is no doubt that God was working in a ceaseless, mighty way. Here they were offering to let me say whatever I wanted, no restrictions at all. Needless to say, I accepted their offer and did the interview.

As the day wore on, we were able to find some time, between phone calls and interviews, to talk about funeral details. In retrospect, this was a rather peculiar conversation. You're sitting there talking about something you never thought possible, which is a terribly surreal thing. At the same time, you're almost glad to be discussing it because you know the funeral will bring some needed closure. Like everything else with this incident, it was like strolling into completely foreign territory. I felt lost and without a map or even a good idea where we were going.

Anyway, for some reason it seemed important to me to hold the funeral in our little church. Unfortunately, the amount of attention we were already receiving suggested we would need a larger venue. Jason was so young and his death so shocking that I knew there would be a ton of family and friends who wanted to attend. I've found, over the years as a pastor, that when a young person dies the funeral is almost always large. Furthermore, I was beginning to realize that there was a need for the community to be involved. In such a small town, everyone had been affected one way or another. I knew that the community (or at least part of it) would want to have the opportunity to get some closure themselves.

We began to brainstorm and several ideas were born. One idea I liked was that maybe we could broadcast the service to the high school. Unfortunately, we were informed this was not a very good option. It became a very difficult problem to deal with. Part of me was saying, "We've been through a terrible loss and I just can't worry about this." My other half knew God was calling us to operate unselfishly. I knew He had some healing He wanted to do in many people. We couldn't just ignore everyone else because we were hurting, and I knew it was vital that we do things God's way. I felt like I was between the proverbial rock and a hard place, but as the day wore on, more discussion and prayer finally yielded an answer.

The only plausible solution was to hold the funeral *and* a large memorial service. This created another concern for me. How do you get through both of these emotionally charged and difficult events?

The only practical way to do things was to have both on the same day. That meant another seemingly endless day for my already battered family. In the end, I realized that the Lord had carried us this far and He wasn't about to drop us now. The Lord also very strongly impressed upon my heart that we needed to hold the memorial service at the high school. I phoned up our friend and parishioner, Sharon Holtman. She was on the school board at that time. I informed her that we would like to have the memorial service at the school. I also said I was planning on going to the spot where Jason fell, to pray. After checking with the rest of the board she let me know that this was fine.

In addition to all this planning, Friday was also a day of many more tears and faces at the door. There were so many helpful people, I wish to thank them all. I must point out one lady, Deb Phillips, who really blessed us. We knew her from New Life Church across town. She had come by the house on Thursday. Deb decided that it was her job to come to our house for the next few days and serve us any way she could. She answered phones (which was no small task because we have two lines in our house, church and private, and as I have already explained, they were ringing literally every couple of minutes), prepared and served food, cleaned, and just did anything she could to help. We really appreciated Deb and her teenager's faithful support day after day.

I know it was crucial for people like Deb to be around because, like Thursday, a constant stream of people started flowing through the house by mid-morning and continued until late evening. If I had to guess, I would bet that at least 300 people a day were sweeping through the house. This included the majority of our extended family who had mostly arrived by Friday. Diane's mom was one of them, and it was again a time of profuse weeping. Two of her brothers had also arrived with their families and that definitely helped. Diane's dad had passed away in 1983 of cancer so it was good to have brothers around. In such broken times you can never have enough loving family. It was good to see them all.

Another visitor we received that day was a teacher from the high school. This particular visit revealed just *how many* people had been *directly* affected by Jason's death. You see, when the shooter entered the school he had encountered this teacher. She was racked and bound by guilt because she had not been able to stop the incident. You could just see the immense pain in her eyes. Tears began to flow as she talked, and they were hot with tormented emotion. So Diane and I did our best to alleviate this false guilt that was attacking her. Like everyone else we saw that day, we gave her a hug and some reassurance. I pray that the Lord has set her free from those feelings of culpability. In the craziness of everything, I had not realized the full extent of people who were severely afflicted by this event.

It wasn't long after our visit with this teacher that the school superintendent dropped in. Our friend, Sharon Holtman, was with him. They wanted to do anything they could for us. They even insisted that the school board would look after all funeral costs. We were very thankful for the offer, but I also felt bad for them. Having been so helpless to prevent such a terrible atrocity in one of their schools must have been a difficult thing to deal with.

Eventually they left and I got up to look out our front window. There were still several people busy milling around. Visiting, crying, and hugging had become commonplace in our home. I peered out the window at Jason's car, which I had parked out front the night of his death. I don't know how much time elapsed as I stood there vacantly. I was just lost in thought until another vehicle pulled up. I remember watching a teenage boy and girl get out of the vehicle. The girl delicately placed a carnation under the driver's side wiper blade of Jason's car. Yet again the emotions burst through the surface and tears caressed my cheek. To this day I don't know who they were but I want them to know I appreciated that gesture. We left the carnation there until after the memorial service.

Friday also brought our good friend, Jim Berkley, to town. Just a month prior, Jim had been the guest speaker for our parish conference. He was in the middle of leading another conference when he heard about Jason's untimely death. Shortly after receiving the news, he felt the Lord tell him to come and be with us. This was passed on to the people at the conference, and after some prayer, they all agreed. A collection was taken up and Jim was soon on a plane headed for our area.

I had come to know Jim as a friend during my prior experiences with him. He was, and is, a warrior for God with a wonderful prophetic gifting. It was comforting to know he was on the way. I had looked forward to seeing him again. So when Jim appeared at the front door that day, the now commonplace wet tears and warm hugs ensued. He and I then retreated into my study just off the front entryway. We chatted for a little while but then Jim cut right to the heart of things. He asked me two questions I will never forget. There is no doubt that the Lord sent him to ask me these difficult questions. I remember Jim peering out from his round face and saying, "Of course you know that Jason is with the Lord in Heaven now."

"Yes, I know that," I quietly responded.

"Well, I want you to ask yourself one question. Do you think he wants to come back?" Jim's resolute eyes gazed at me from across the study.

"No," I said after a painful pause. "I'm sure he doesn't want to come back."

The revelatory light bulb once again lit up. On an intellectual level it was an easy answer. What we don't realize is that our intellect is often a thousand miles from our heart. That question forced me to examine my own heart closely. The experience was absolutely wrenching and yet very soothing. It had been necessary to bridge the chasm between the two.

As I sat there pondering, tears once again washed my face in a deluge of passion. I certainly, beyond a shadow of a doubt, wanted Jason back. I would have given just about anything in that moment to have him back. But I was also finally and absolutely certain that he was in the indescribable presence of the Lord. There is no way anyone would want to leave that. This epiphany allowed me some peace. It was difficult to admit that Jason wouldn't be coming back, or would even want to. But it gave me peace to understand intellectually and *heartfully* that he was in Paradise with Jesus. Looking back, there was nothing anyone could have said to stop the pain of losing our son. However, that one question has been and continues to this day to be a source of comfort.

There were also other comforts that pointed to Jason's place in Paradise. Three separate people came to us, independently of one another, and shared dreams they felt they had been given. In all three there was great joy and Jason was in Paradise. I realize many people are skeptical of dreams and visions. There is need for careful discernment to ascertain whether something is actually from the Lord. However, that is material for an entirely different book. Suffice to say it was nice to hear of those dreams. I really do think they were from the Lord and they helped ease our pain a little.

The summer of 1998 is another of these comforts. It was this summer that our youth went on a mission trip to Tijuana, Mexico. They built a home for a family there and did some street ministry. The Lord had really moved and touched many of the kids. Jason was one of those kids significantly impacted and he had recommitted his life to Jesus. Sadly, it's easy to become dry and lukewarm as Christians. But that trip had been a time of renewal for many of the kids and I thank God Jason was there. Regardless, I take comfort knowing where Jason is and thinking about a timeless place where the family will be whole again. There is no doubt about it. Praise God!

The flurry of activity that Friday kept rolling along. There was one last unexpected visitor. Archbishop Barry Curtis (the head of my Anglican diocese) had made the journey from Calgary. I had a long vein of history with this man. Working at St. James, I had occasionally crossed paths with him right from the beginning. Then after graduating from seminary he had ordained me in Taber. We'd had a cordial relationship through all those years. Even though we didn't see eye to eye on many issues, he'd always been honest and open with me.

And there we were, paths intertwining once again, him standing at our door with the indescribable pain of our loss chiselled on his face. He was a very compassionate man. I'd seen him at other funerals in the past and I knew this kind of loss was very difficult for him. Unfortunately, he had already announced his retirement. This incident was going to go down as a rather dark chapter in his ministry. He stayed with us for around an hour that day and I appreciated his support and care. In the end, Friday, like Wednesday and Thursday, was a day of tears. But more importantly, it was a day of revelation and blessing. God had continued to bless us with His peace and manifest presence. He had touched many lives once again.

Saturday, May 1

Rest continued to be a difficult commodity to come by in our household. Somehow, though, I managed to fall asleep late Friday night, hoping to sleep until a reasonable time the next morning. Yet again my hopes went unfulfilled. But this time it was a pleasant awakening. It was about 6:30 that morning when the Lord nudged me to consciousness. This had happened on Friday morning also and it would happen again on Sunday. I would not clearly understand what was going on until then. It was a pleasant awakening as I said, but I can't say that I was particularly pleased to be awake at that hour.

I look back now and I am very thankful the Lord did what He did. That was the only time during those insane days that I could really be alone with Him. And He was waking me up each morning to give me a sermon for the memorial service. It wasn't until Sunday when I received the final part that the puzzle came together. The talk was to start with a segment about Jason, the kind of person he was and what his life was like. I would then, after wading through this emotional subject, move on to the topic of evil. Here I would talk about what had really happened and why. I would also look at the problem from a national and global perspective. During this time, I planned on going to the spot where Jason died, to pray. The third part, which I received Sunday, was the answer to the incredibly difficult questions raised during the talk – Jesus. Specifically, that Jesus is the source of all love, and that we desperately need such love and respect for one another. It's the only way to stop the hurt, anger, and violence.

The Lord has given me many things to say over the years, but His intense presence during these three mornings was profound. He just flowed through the room, thick like honey, during those intimate encounters. His presence was so focused and direct. Afterward, as the weeks and months passed, many people have shared with me how penetrating those words were at the memorial service. How substantially they and people they knew had been impacted. Glory to God, because nothing I could ever have said would have had near the impact or wisdom without His anointing.

By now I was starting to get used to all the visitors and Saturday was no different. Amidst all of this, I knew that I needed to prepare for my Sunday services at the church. There was just no way that the regular services could go on like normal. In many ways, I simply didn't want to lead the congregation at all. I was well beyond exhausted and just didn't feel I could do the Sunday services with two more looming on Monday.

I've learned many things about leadership over the years. One of the most crucial is that real leaders will continue to lead through the toughest circumstances. They persevere and lead even when they don't feel like it. Here I was, in the blackest days of my short life, called to be a pastor of a little Anglican church in Taber, Alberta. It was now, more than ever, that I needed to do what God had called me to do.

After praying and talking to Di about it, I decided there would be only one Sunday service instead of two. I would lead the congregation in a time of worship and prayer. I didn't feel called to preach and there wouldn't be any communion. I thank God that He is constantly trying to teach us to walk in *His* strength rather than our weakness. Even though I still often try to do things my way, I knew that I couldn't have led that congregation at all the next day. But I was at peace because I also knew the Lord would carry us.

The memorial service and funeral also had to be planned Saturday. Mike Rose and I discussed these difficult arrangements that morning. I really can't say enough about Mike during this time in my life. He is a man of great faith who sincerely loves the Lord, and he has a wonderful servile heart. His sincere care and love for our family shone through brightly during the whole ordeal. He was the second person at the hospital after Jason died. Since that time he hadn't left my side, supporting me and praying for me. What an immeasurable blessing to have that kind of assistance from a friend.

Anyway, we started by discussing the memorial service. I realized that we needed to have someone preside over it, besides me. Doug Shimoda (the pastor of New Life Church in Taber) was the obvious choice. New Life's congregation had been a blessing to us over the years and we had close ties with them. I knew Doug fairly well and trusted him as a close friend. So, as mid-morning approached, Mike and I made the short jaunt over to his house. Once there, I asked Doug to preside over the memorial service and he quickly agreed. The three of us then began to hash out the details of who would do what. We began to pray and talk amongst each other. Through this, it became apparent that we needed to involve as many local pastors as possible. I really appreciated the support from the entire body of Christ in our community.

Somewhere in the midst of this process, Doug and I both began noticing that Mike was making little noises. This didn't register with me at first because Mike tends to make funny faces and noises occasionally. Eventually I could no longer ignore his odd behaviour and I had to ask. You never know what kind of an answer you're going to get. Little did I realize that the Lord had him in the middle of a vision. So, without knowing, I asked what was going on.

"It's like there is an Imax screen in front of me and I can see them coming all the way to the horizon. I can't even count them, there's so many!" Mike answered.

"Huh?" was the only thought that crossed my mind. So I responded, "What are you talking about, what is it that you are seeing?"

"Angels," he said as he continued to stare off into space. "There are countless thousands upon thousands of angels pouring into

Taber." His face lit up and seemed to glow. It was becoming increasingly clear that God was using Jason's death in a mighty way. We had struggled for years to bring light into this little town. Now it was being bombarded with God's presence. It was as if a veil had been torn off from above the town and the Heavens were now open over Taber. Many people, Christians included, are either completely unaware or just don't care about the spiritual warfare that goes on in our lives everyday. Yet there was no way we were going to be able to ignore what was going on here, and thank God for that. This vision of Mike's was just one more reminder of this.

Upon finishing the memorial service details, I headed home to pick up Di. We needed to go down to the funeral home and arrange things. Neither of us looked forward to that visit. As a pastor, I have spent more time than I care to reflect on in that funeral home. Thankfully, a man by the name of Terry Reardon was the director and we had become friends throughout the years. Terry is quite gifted at dealing with people who have experienced loss and he was very gracious and helpful to us. That still didn't ease the pain of going over our son's funeral arrangements, but it was comforting to have a friend going over it with us.

Every detail we discussed felt like a brick smacking my chest, knocking the wind out of me. Picking out a casket proved to be an especially excruciating experience. It was just so wrong and still very surreal. I would catch myself thinking, when am I going to wake up? This just isn't right, how can we pick out a casket for *our* son? With great difficulty we eventually decided on a nice casket that we thought suited Jason.

Before long it was time to choose a plot at the Taber Memorial Gardens. I wasn't sure then and I'm definitely not sure now – but for some reason, Diane and I reserved two spaces beside Jason's. We had never planned on spending the rest of our lives anywhere near Taber. And yet, the thought of our son's physical body being buried there compelled us to reserve spots for ourselves. When it was over, planning our son's funeral felt like someone was rubbing salt into our gaping wounds. We survived, though, and headed home knowing that there was one less thing to do.

People were still bustling around answering phones and doorbells as we arrived home. We quickly settled back into the activity of the house. Then came an unexpected call. It was the father of the boy who had shot our Jason. In situations like this, nobody gets away unaffected. That man fought through a myriad of tears and bared his broken heart to me throughout the conversation. It was much of what you would expect, I guess. He said how sorry he was and expressed his sympathy. He wished he could have taken the bullet in Jason's place.

I say that it was much of what you would expect because there really is nothing that can be said. God blessed me at several points throughout this tragedy with words, but really you can't express the weeping of your spirit verbally. However, I very much appreciated this man's attempt to express his sorrow and I accepted his genuine apology. I thanked him for his words and then there was silence. We both realized that there was nothing else to be said. This conversation deeply stirred me and I couldn't imagine being in that father's shoes. Again, I was intensely aware that our family and friends were not the only people in great pain through this ordeal.

Thankfully, Saturday was not solely defined by pain – there were blessings as well. First, the e-mails continued to flood in and the prayer support was incredible. As well, God's hand was all over everything, even the little details. No, I would say God was especially taking care of the little details. You can't imagine what an amazing relief and blessing this was for us. Caught in the hurricane of our situation, we just didn't have the time or energy for minor details. Incredibly, He was providing for every last little thing we could think of.

Earlier in the day, Diane had mentioned that she really didn't have anything to wear to the memorial service. We had no idea if we would find time to remedy that. It normally wouldn't have been a big deal with Di. But when it's your son's memorial, it becomes an important thing. Then our friend, Alison Chinn, stopped in. I don't know whom she had talked to or how it came about, but she had three new dresses with her. They were from a local store and Diane was told she could choose any one of them as a gift for her to wear. The one Diane liked fit perfectly and she looked radiant in it.

I also received a call from the owner of an upscale men's clothing store in Lethbridge. He said that he would be honoured to give us a new suit for the burial. Jason had never worn a suit in his life. Actually, it was a minor tussle just getting him to wear a sport coat. He was your typical teenager in that sense and was definitely not a suit guy. This is mind, we decided not to take up this generous offer. We graciously thanked the man and explained that we just couldn't see Jason in a suit.

It was little blessings like these, even the ones we didn't take advantage of, that really helped us through. I would just like to say thank you to everyone who blessed us, prayed for, and supported us. God's grace was so evident through all of this and I am reminded how well He provides for us.

A provincial employee by the name of Peter also arrived in town that day. It was one more way the Lord was taking care of us. Premier Ralph Klein had sent him with instructions to make sure that basically we got whatever we wanted. He was there to take care of details so that we didn't have to.

It had been decided at some point that the memorial service would be broadcast on television. Two news networks were going to air it live across the country. To be honest, I have no recollection of being asked if this could happen. Nevertheless, the Lord gave me a peace about it and I knew it was fine. I would, of course, later find out that the broadcast had touched many lives. I still meet people today who tell me how significantly they were impacted by it.

Peter dealt with all of the details involved with this. He generally made sure that everything for the memorial service was done just as we wanted. He proved to be very helpful to us over the few days. I would like to thank him for his help. I must say, though, it was a bit odd having the Premier of Alberta send someone to us in little Taber. But, in the wake of everything else, it fit right in.

Finally, Saturday came to an end. Hundreds more people had entered our home and the phones had continued to ring. The common thread through this whole ordeal had been pain and Saturday provided her share. Funeral and memorial service arrangements had taken their toll. God's grace and blessing, the other common thread, also continued to be woven through several lives during this time. There had been so many requests and details to sort out. Yet God had faithfully taken care of everything. Most of all, He had continued to bless our family with His incredible presence in ways we hadn't known before.

Sunday, May 2

The Lord woke me early on Sunday. In the calm serenity of the wee morning hours, I remember just lying there in silence, another day looming before me. I recall thinking that maybe today would be less painful than the past three or four. Maybe it was a naïve thought and maybe it was just deep-seated wishful thinking. Either way, Sunday was going to be one of the most painful days.

After considerable coaxing, I was eventually able to pry my body from the warm environment of my bed. I began milling around the house, engulfed by what now seemed to be a permanent dreamlike haze. One by one, other members of the family began to get up. I started thinking about the morning service. I had no idea how the Lord was going to pull me through it. Mentally, I was just completely out of it and I was equally inept physically. I've heard insomniacs talk about what happens when you can't sleep for days on end. You get to this glossed-over dream-like state where you're never really awake and yet never asleep. That is exactly how this "haze" felt – as if a dark cloud had settled around me and I couldn't find my way through it. Everything seemed to be in slow motion and I can remember feeling totally overwhelmed.

I was still lost in thought when the phone broke the glassy morning silence. It was one of several calls we would receive from media people wanting to attend our service. Most of them just wanted to observe, but one crew asked if they could bring a camera. As graciously as I could, I told them they couldn't bring the camera in but that they were welcome to come. I didn't want our personal worship to become some sort of media circus. As a church family, we needed more than ever to concentrate on and worship our God, to just chase after and sit in His presence. I was afraid that a bunch of cameras would make it very difficult for people to focus on the Lord. They needed to be free in their expression of worship.

I walked apprehensively to the church that morning. Thinking about it now, I really can't say why. Probably because I was just so exhausted. The service was just one more thing that could've ended up draining me even more. I can't say for sure though, because in my spirit I knew I needed to be there and wanted to be there.

The congregation slowly filtered in that morning alongside a trickle of media people. Many hugs were exchanged as people entered the building. I remember very clearly the atmosphere in the church that morning. Sadness filled every eye and a vapour of sorrow wafted around the room. I began the service with a prayer and decided to move straight into worship.

Worship is one of the most effective ways to release God's presence. It is such a powerful thing when approached with a humble heart. Scripture says that God will not deny a broken heart and contrite spirit. We definitely had broken hearts and contrite spirits that day and the peace of God broke out in that place powerfully. The sorrow didn't leave but it was now mixed with the peace and joy of God. As we continued to worship, I realized how much I needed to verbally express the heaviness of my spirit. Singing and crying out to the Lord through worship was an incredible part of my grieving. The Lord just began melting the burdens on my heart as I sang. I would find over the next several weeks that times of worship would often transform into times of release and grieving.

Eventually the worship began to wind down. I wanted to just stay in that place of worship for the rest of my time here on this earth.

But sadly it ended, and I knew it was time to move into a significant period of prayer. I had removed the liturgical aspects of our service, which is the structure we usually move with (though the Lord frequently leads us off our liturgical path). So I began to lead the church into a time of prayer.

We began by praying for the world in general. I encouraged the congregation to join in and cry out to the Lord. Eventually we wound our way through the nation's needs and then Taber's needs. Inevitably we began praying for our church and then our family. Continuing along this path we prayed for the boy who shot Jason and his family. Finally we began to pray specifically for Jason. Once again a hurricane of grief and emotion broke through the surface and overwhelmed me. I knelt on the stairs at the front of our church, warm tears bathing my face. I knelt there completely unable to control my emotions. The reality of Jason's death was overpowering and unyielding. Before long I felt an arm around my shoulder. Mike Rose had walked up to the front and knelt down beside me. One by one the rest of the congregation began to follow Mike's lead.

I look back now and realize how *very* right this was. We were all in this together. We had all suffered a loss. The church family had watched Jason grow from the innocent and tender age of five into an honourable young man of seventeen. They had loved him very much.

I don't know how long we all stayed there weeping together at the front of the church. We all needed to share our tears with one another, to lean on one another. The media kept their distance, of course, and I'm sure they didn't know how to take all of this. But I pray that God planted seeds in those people that morning. After this time of weeping finally ended, we sang a few more songs and closed with a short prayer.

One thing I really noticed on Sunday was the media. They seemed to be everywhere, even more so than the previous three days. As I walked home from the church that day, there were several people shooting pictures and camera footage from across the street. Then, sitting in my house, I could see media types up and down the block. I began to wonder what it was like to have their job. They often have to cover terrible stories and are frequently not well received. I can definitely understand the friction between the reporters of the news and those caught in the crossfire of it.

Early that afternoon, a small group of these reporters came to the door and asked if they could speak with me. So I invited them in, answered a few questions, and made a few comments. As I looked around that room at their faces I saw the sadness in their tear-filled eyes. It really struck me that they're just people like the rest of us, regardless of their job. That sounds obvious and simple, but it's so easy to think of them as less than that. I know the media takes a lot of criticism when they cover situations like ours. But I can only tell you that they were very respectful of my family throughout the whole ordeal.

After the media cleared out, the house seemed strangely empty. Only the family and a few close friends were present. Deb Phillips and her children were still serving and helping any way they could. We really appreciated that. Still, compared to the continuous river of people from the previous three days, it seemed unusually quiet. This really was a welcome break, but at the same time I felt just a little bit sadder. All the insane busyness had kept us somewhat distracted. The quiet of Sunday afternoon somehow gave the reality of Jason's death a more sharp and painful bite.

About mid-afternoon, I decided to take a drive over to the high school. Preparations for the next day's memorial service were busily underway. The CTV and CBC news networks were planning on broadcasting the service live. They had also arranged to have a large screen set up in the gym. That way a cameraman could follow us as we went to pray where Jason had been shot. If all went according to plan, everyone in the gym would still be able to see and hear what was going on. Peter had everything firmly under control with only a few details that needed to be ironed out.

Everything seemed fine so I walked out of the school into the warm playful sunshine. It's funny how God reminds you of things. I can remember looking at Jason's shiny black Camaro (which I had driven over to the school) and being reminded of a prophetic word from a month earlier. In late March our church had its annual conference and the guest speaker that year had been the aforementioned Jim Berkley. The weekend turned out to be a wonderful time of learning and growing with the Lord. During this time, Jim had spoken an interesting prophetic word over me. It was now ringing in my ears again, as if he was right there.

He had said vehemently, "There are young people waiting to hear from you, Dale – teenagers and young adults." At the time, I thought that Jim was not hearing clearly from Lord. I spent years working with young people but Mike Rose was now doing that work in our church. I definitely did not feel called to move back to it. Standing there looking at the Camaro I realized how wrong I was. Tomorrow I would be speaking to some 450 high school students. Countless more people would see it across Canada via television. That was just the beginning, as I have now spoken in over 200 schools to some 80,000 teens. You just never know where God will take you.

As the evening crept closer, my emotions began to swell again. I knew that we would be headed to the funeral home to view the body. I don't think anybody really wanted to go through with this, but we all knew that it was painfully necessary. When the time arrived, Jason's two closest friends and most of the family drove over to the funeral home. Everybody was ghastly silent as we entered the room where Jason's body lay. I remember kind of creeping and sliding up to the casket. I really didn't want to look in. When I did look, what I saw was not my son. It didn't look like him. It was at best a bad caricature of Jason. I knew then just how temporary these physical bodies are. This was not my son lying before me; it was simply the body that carried and housed him for seventeen years. Now that he was no longer there, it really didn't look like him at all. As other family members came up, many, many more tears were shed. The funeral home had taken Jason's last school picture and blown it up to poster size for the memorial service. Through my tears, I noticed it there to the side of the casket. I quickly realized that it was much easier for me to look at this picture of Jason than to look at his remains. Meanwhile, Jason's brothers and his friends had all written notes and they placed them in the casket. It was so hard for them and we were all thankful to exit that room. All I can say is that this topped off what had already been another painful day. Thinking of how hard it was being in that funeral home, it amazes me that the Lord still worked through us during the whole ordeal.

Driving home that evening, I realized how strange the world seemed to me. The lens through which I looked had now been inexorably stained and tinted. The grass no longer seemed so green and the sky was not nearly as blue. But it wasn't all negative because God seemed somehow more close, even though I know He'd always been there. It was now obvious to me that my priorities badly needed readjustment. The rest of the evening was quiet and restful, but I knew it was only that eye of the storm I had so longed for on Friday.

Monday, May 3

In the still of the morning, the air was cool and refreshing, quite peaceful. The sun was out in full force and it promised to be a beautiful day. It would have been nice to sit and enjoy the calm that morning, or maybe even be out for a balloon flight. This unfortunately was no ordinary day. It was Monday, May 3, 1999. On this day we would bury Jason, our third son.

The calm of the morning was quickly lost as the house came alive with activity. People were scrambling around to get ready for the memorial service. Simultaneously, members of our extended family were arriving at the door. My sister was among them, having come in from Vernon, British Columbia, and she was a welcome sight. Diane's brother Glenn, his wife Sue, and their three daughters had been busy preparing the church for the funeral. We really cherished their greatly needed help. All in all, it was already a hectic day and we hadn't even left for the memorial service.

The bizarre feeling that had accompanied this whole ordeal was more pronounced than ever. The fact that Premier Klein, Mrs. Chrétien, and Preston Manning were going to be in attendance didn't help that feeling. It just didn't seem to make sense, all of these national figures in our little town. Of course, speaking at my son's memorial didn't either.

Eventually several limousines pulled up to the front of the house. We had arranged for Jason's Camaro to be parked out front of the school waiting for us. It just seemed somehow to be the right thing to do. The family began piling into the limousines and soon we were off. A long trail of extended family followed as we left the house. I had not ridden in a limousine in a long time and I couldn't think of a worse reason to be riding in one now.

Passing through town, many people stopped whatever they were doing and just stared as we drove by. This only added to the mounting surrealistic feeling that was pervading every corner of my mind. Thankfully, it wasn't a long drive and we arrived at the school in short time. Upon entering, we were quickly ushered off into the boardroom to wait. You could have heard pins drop in that room. Gazing around, I saw raw emotion chiselled on every face. My parents' long, sad faces especially struck me and I wondered where they found the energy to march on. This had been an indescribable drain on everyone. I can't imagine how high the toll must have been for them at their ages.

My thoughts were invaded as someone entered the room. They wanted to introduce us to the dignitaries before we started the service. Again we were ushered, this time to the school office, and we shook hands with these folks, mostly politicians. They all offered their sympathies and you could see the birth of a tear in every eye. Premier Klein was the only one not there. He was late arriving and we were pressed for time, so they decided to start the service.

I really wish that I was better with words, but even then I don't believe I could describe how hard it was to walk into that gym. Words are simply inadequate for many things in life and they fall woefully short here. Entering the gym, I could see that large and luminous picture of Jason resting at the front. It was a bit overwhelming to have this huge picture of him watch us walk in. I could also literally feel the intense collective gaze of the crowd probing the family and me. Their eyes were desperately searching. Searching for answers to questions they didn't even know how to ask. Their curiosity of how we would react to this situation would soon be satisfied. Reaching the front row, we sat down and Pastor Doug began the service.

The opening welcome was slightly uncomfortable due to the sombre nature of the service. But things changed quickly as we flowed into a song. New Life's worship team had graciously accepted our request to provide music for the service. We were very careful about what songs were chosen. We didn't want a bunch of dark, sombre funeral dirges. Jason was in Heaven, and as much as it hurt to lose him, we knew that he was better off. So we wanted some upbeat, happier music. This really was a time for celebration and mourning. I know that this may sound oddly paradoxical to you. But when you have *real* revelation (as opposed to intellectual/emotional reasoning) of what it *means* to be at the Father's side in Heaven, part of you can't help but celebrate. Thankfully, we knew where Jason was and that was a reason to praise if ever I had one.

Many of the questions we would receive in the weeks after the service focused on this very thing. Why would you sing and clap your hands like that at a memorial service? It is a joy to be able to share with people whenever that is asked of me. I know that God has used it to plant many seeds. When someone has an intimate, personal relationship with the Lord, funerals and memorial services should take on a whole different meaning. Trust me, people will notice. They wonder why it is so much different for that family, and that is exactly what God did with us. The presence of God was released in that place as we sang that first song, and I knew God was busy at work in many hearts.

After the opening music, the service continued with a steady ebb and flow of speakers. This included the principal of the school and Jason's two best friends, Matthew Pollock and Dustin Bell. Both Matt and Dustin had nervously consented to say a few words. I told them just to speak what was on their hearts. It didn't have to be some worn-out cliché or fancy speech. They went up together, hesitantly making their way to the podium. Before long they were pouring out their hearts about Jason and how they would miss him. What a blessing it was to me for those guys to share like that – thank you both. After these speakers, there was another song and then a few pastors read different pieces of Scripture.

As the last Scripture was read, I became very aware that it was time for me to speak. I slowly walked up to the front and turned on the lapel microphone. The Lord had given me what to say, and now, cutting through the mix of pain and joy was His awesome peace. It was a peace that I needed to share with all of these people. I started by talking about the kind of person Jason was. He never liked to see people bullied or picked on. Sadly, it had been a bullied young man who had killed him. This seemed so bitterly ironic to me as I spoke. I could almost taste the bitter metallic tang of irony on the end of my tongue. Thankfully, as I continued to talk of Jason and his soft malleable heart, the taste quickly left.

Continuing on, I began to discuss the evil that had come into all our lives. This point had been undeniably driven home a day earlier. During a visit, several students had stated they earnestly never wanted to set foot in that school again. Pausing my talk, I realized we needed to go and pray over the spot where Jason had fallen. I looked at my wife and headed out of the gym. The family, along with Matthew, Dustin, and a cameraman, followed as I went past the office to the spot where Jason died. Arriving, we stood there for a moment, just looking at the floor. This was the last thing my son saw before he lost consciousness for the final time. I began to pray forcefully from my spirit. I cast evil out of that place in the name of Jesus. I prayed that this moment would be the beginning of taking back the school from fear and evil. We concluded the prayer and walked back to the gymnasium.

I finished by addressing the students of Myers. I challenged them to have the safest school on the planet. I told them that if everyone who attended Myers felt accepted and respected, it would be a safe place. If they genuinely cared for one another, it could be the safest school in the nation. I spoke from Romans chapter 5 where Paul tells us a couple of key things. First, that while we are being tested in this life, our faith and perseverance will build character in us. Second, he says that God has poured out His love into our hearts by the Holy Spirit. I said that it was love that would change the world – God's love living in us. I could see many faces covered in tears as I concluded my talk.

As I finished, the service proceeded with our sister-in-law, Melanie McMurray, singing a powerful song about Heaven. They began to show some pictures and video footage of Jason as she sang. Most of it was taken during the mission trip to Tijuana, Mexico. How painful it was to see our son so full of potential, a smile on his face in almost every shot. Those images will remain in my memory forever.

With everything finished, Doug thanked those in attendance and I stood up to end the service with a prayer. I hadn't planned what to pray ahead of time. I just relied on the Lord to lead it. Praise God, because that closing prayer created significant ripples on the national pond. I started by simply praying for our world. Then I began to pray for the boy who shot Jason. In that prayer I forgave him and I encouraged the community to forgive him and support the family. To this day, people still ask me how I could forgive him. The truth is, only through the love of God was I able to. But it was this particular act of forgiving him that really made people stand up and take notice of our situation. It really made them wonder why we acted the way we did.

After the prayer we sang a closing song and exited the gym. A reception was planned for the school cafeteria and we headed there. The room filled quickly and was soon jammed with people. What a blessing to be able to share about God with all of those folks. It didn't matter what they asked, really. Because inevitably any question regarding our situation revolved around God so the answer always found its way there. At one point I clearly remember seeing my wife give Madame Chrétien a big hug. I chuckled because somehow it seemed out of place, here, being the Prime Minister's wife and all. I think she really needed it though, and appreciated my wife's comfort. As we finally left, there was the usual throng of media. We briskly answered a few questions before leaving. Looking back, it was through the memorial service that God carried me the most. There is no way it could have been done otherwise.

Being so depleted, it would have been nice if there was some time between the memorial service and funeral. But we barely had time to catch our breath before the funeral service was to start. I remember driving home and seeing my three remaining sons in the Camaro just behind us. Once again my heartstrings were pulled as I watched them drive their departed brother's new car. It was so hard on all of us.

The funeral was going to be a whole different ball game. I had focused what little time and energy I had on planning the memorial service. Thus, the funeral would turn out to be less organized. We had restricted it to family and close friends but our little church was still bursting at the seams. Only 100 could actually sit in the church itself; and there were 400 more people in the upper and lower halls watching via closed circuit television. Bishop Barry was in attendance to preside over the service. Also our good friends, Reverend Charles Alexander and Reverend John Torley, were there, and both spoke. The funeral also had a lot more music in it. We had filled it with upbeat, contemporary worship songs. I have longed for Christians to use upbeat music at funerals when the person has gone to Paradise. The service seemed to go by in a flash, and everything went smoothly in spite of my lack of planning.

Next we proceeded to the Taber Memorial Gardens for graveside prayers. Terry Reardon, the funeral director, had nicely prepared the site for us. Over 300 people came out to the graveyard. The surrealistic feeling I was experiencing had now progressed into full-fledged dream mode. I had conducted dozens of internments out here but none of this seemed real. The previous days had been so difficult, and yet this moment took the cake with ease. It's during this time that the reality and permanence of your loss knocks you off your feet. As the casket was lowered, it felt like someone was pulling my heart from my chest. I remember that my son, Mark, began weeping at the sight of the casket disappearing. He had kept his composure for most of the day but the cruel finality of this was too much. I wish I could have traded places with Jason. I so much wanted to, but then it struck me what a selfish thought that was. Jason was in Paradise now and wouldn't return even if he could. I knew we'd see him again, and as I thought about this, it made it easier to cope as the internment finished.

Afterwards we went home to collect ourselves before heading to the Heritage Hotel. This site was chosen for the reception mainly because of its size. We arrived at the hotel and for whatever reason, Diane and I ended up standing a ways apart. Before we knew it, two lines just formed out of nowhere. We spent the entire reception just hugging and crying with people. We saw so many wonderful family and friends from many different eras in our lives. In particular, I was especially blessed by a large contingent of balloonists from Calgary. Many of these folks I have known for over twenty-five years. Balloonists tend to be a fairly tight-knit community. I was glad that they took the time out of their crazy schedules to be with us. It's funny because so often we let the busyness of life control us and we don't make time for people. I have never heard of anyone, at the end of their life, say that they regretted not getting enough work done. Yet, I have heard people express regrets of not spending enough time with people, family, and friends. When my time here is finished I don't want that kind of regret.

As the reception wound down, the cries of my body became audible to me. I was exhausted and I felt beaten and bruised. We went home knowing we were undeservedly blessed people and a little relieved that the day was over. Most of all we were tired, worn, and sorrowful. There were still a number of relatives at the house that evening but it was quiet. We sat around talking and sometimes laughing. But still, the redolence of grief choked the air.

Tuesday, May 4

I am including a short section on this day, Tuesday, because it was the first day back to school since the shooting. Diane and I had asked to be in the school that morning to help the students any way we could. Thankfully, the administration had agreed to this suggestion of our attendance – although I'm pretty sure they weren't completely comfortable with it. I guess they were as unsure of what would transpire that morning as we were. So as the sun rose on another day, Di and I did the same. It was another exceptionally quiet morning as everyone else was still sleeping. Neither Matt nor Jen, who were both still in school, would be going that morning. They were just as exhausted as we were and definitely not ready to face a day back at school.

The morning air was crisp and refreshing, even to *my* weary bones. We arrived quite early so that we would beat any students there, though I'm sure none of them were in a rush to get to school. After speaking with some of the staff and crisis counsellors, we decided to stand close to where Jason was shot. We felt that it would be very difficult for some students to walk that hallway. I must admit, it felt kind of odd just standing there in that empty school, so close to where our son had perished. Before long, the first students entered the school. Soon they began to approach us, some by themselves, but usually in small groups. It just seemed natural to hug these students and comfort them, so that's what we did. At the time I knew how much Diane and I needed those hugs, but looking back, I now realize that some of those students needed them even more.

Some of the crisis counsellors stood off at a distance and just watched. They looked puzzled and weren't sure what to make of this situation. The woman who had been in the hospital was there and she looked especially uncomfortable with this. Several times she came over to talk to Diane, but in general she kept her distance. As we expected, there were a number of students who were having trouble walking past the spot where the shooting occurred. The teachers graciously brought these students to us and we walked them down the hall to their classrooms. Most of them were in tears so we did what we could to comfort them and allay their fears. That morning we greeted and hugged over 300 young people. It was just one more step in the slow but steady healing process, for them and us.

After we finished at the school, we headed to our house knowing we had a busy afternoon ahead. The television show "100 Huntley Street" (Canada's longest running Christian program) had called and asked if they could come out and do an interview. One of the show's hosts, Lorna Dueck, had offered to come out from Ontario to interview the family. We weren't sure whether or not to do the interview – everyone was exhausted and tired of all the activity. After praying about it, though, we felt that it was something the Lord wanted us to do. The Huntley Street crew arrived that morning and began setting up their equipment. They had to rearrange our living room for the interview, so it took a while for them to be ready. Lorna was very gracious, sensitive, and likable. I think that made all of us more comfortable. I chuckled to myself watching my sons wince as make-up was applied to their faces for the interview. This was definitely not part of the deal they had bargained for.

Finally, the family gathered around the couch as Lorna conducted a sensible and professional interview. It seemed rather hot under all those lights, but the grace of God prevailed again and the interview went well. We would receive many cards and letters from people across the country who said they were blessed by the show. Jenny was the only member of the family who didn't take part. She was still very overwhelmed by everything and didn't want to be on television. She sat on the steps with Deb Phillips and watched as Lorna conducted the interview. They did, however, show pictures of Jenny when they broadcast it. Lorna also spent some time with her before the interview and gave her a little stuffed animal.

The end of the interview marked the beginning of a slowdown. The rushes of adrenaline that had been needed to pull and carry us through began to fade. Even as the unimaginable pace from the last week began to slow, we all knew that somehow things were never going to slow very much. For us, the world was a very different place this week as opposed to last. Changed forever in a split second, there was no way to go back. By the grace of God, and I suspect only by His grace, we would now have to trudge forward down a road we could not have anticipated, nor ever wanted.

The Aftermath

Letters, Letters, Incredible Letters

Things did not return to anything even resembling normalcy for the family. Even with the funeral and memorial behind us, the attention we were receiving was incredible. Needless to say, with the events of that crazy period, our mail exploded to unbelievable quantities. Normally we pick up our mail down the street. But, for at least two weeks after the funeral, it arrived at our door in boxes. That's right, boxes and boxes of cards and letters from all around the country. It was just easier for the post office to deliver directly to us. This response from the nation was overwhelming and almost inconceivable in my mind. We really can't thank everyone enough who sent encouraging letters and cards. We read letter after letter of emotional outpouring. It became part of our daily routine to sit down and try to read through each piece of mail that arrived. Really, it became part of our grieving process and often the kind words emanating from the letters would loose a current of tears.

Another small miracle in this situation was that out of nearly 4,000 pieces of mail, very few were *weird* or strange. There's only one I can vividly remember being blatantly negative. This letter actually arrived several months after Jason's death. I had already been speaking in several venues and this man had seen one of my talks. He felt that I had no right to forgive. Only God had that authority in his opinion. Subsequently, he was upset that I was travelling around talking about forgiveness. He felt that I should be using the mild celebrity I had gained to champion for tougher laws. I felt for this man and I'm sure he's been through a lot of pain in his life. I could literally feel his bitterness jumping off the page. In my response to him, I quoted Jesus on forgiveness. I explained to him that although we do need a good legal system, I was much more interested in preventing people from being hurt than punishing those who had committed crimes. If we address the problems we face and learn about forgiveness, I think there will be far fewer people who need to be punished in the first place. I sincerely hope he read my response and stopped to think about his heart. One will never find peace by holding grudges and thoughts of revenge. Nor will tougher laws alleviate any pain from existing wounds.

It really is amazing when you stop to think about how many people there really are in this world, and that each one has a story to tell. Many of the cards and letters we received were notes of sympathy and condolences. But there were so many filled with people's stories, and how their lives had been affected by ours. Some of the stories were gripping cries for help. They would immediately grab your attention and pull at your heartstrings. Others still were filled with words of astonishment. How did you forgive, on national television, the boy who shot your son? Even more to their amazement was how quickly we were able to forgive. Some of them didn't think it was possible. A few of these precious and amazing stories I will never forget.

One of the earliest letters we received was from a young girl here in Taber. Like many students, she was in school that terrible day and had been deeply affected. Her letter arrived the day after the memorial service. She spoke of how much the service had meant to her and how she had absolutely needed to be there. This was a common sentiment from many of the students, but one comment in her letter particularly caught my attention. "At the memorial service even the mean teachers were hugging each other and hugging students." I didn't know this girl or anything about her and it wasn't so much this statement that grabbed me. It was more the thought that it provoked in my mind – that *numerous* people, many of whom we don't realize, find this world an unfriendly place. It really made me think about how we treat each other. I doubted if any of those teachers realized her sentiments toward them. It also made me wonder how often in my life I might have missed reaching out to someone like that girl.

Another letter we received several weeks later was powerful and touching. The story still stands out in my mind. The poor woman writing the letter had been chronically ill for over twenty years. Over time, the challenges of living with constant pain had battered and worn her down. Finally she had arrived at a place where she saw only one option: taking her life. In her own words, "even the love of my daughter was no longer enough to make me want to live." What a terrible place to arrive at. I can't imagine dealing with twenty years of illness without God. He is my only source of hope and strength. Unfortunately, she had obviously arrived at a place of no hope. Continuing with her letter, she wrote that she had not been in a church for some thirty years and had not prayed in all that time. Then, right in the middle of the formation of plans to kill herself, Jason had been murdered.

I have no doubt it was by divine appointment that she decided to watch the memorial service on television. She cried all the way through the service and when it was finally over, she prayed. Can you imagine? After thirty years she found herself praying through her tears. After thirty years of not talking to God, the barrier was finally smashed by what He was doing with Jason's death. She said, "I prayed for the first time in a long time and I was born again." The changes in her life were utterly amazing. She now felt she had a reason to live. Also the pain that she could no longer bear became manageable. The transformation in this lady's life was so affecting and dramatic that even her close friends did not recognize her. Her countenance had been so lifted and transformed that she looked like a different person. This is her description, not mine. It's amazing how much God did there.

Do you see what a breakthrough this was? In a flash God snatched her from the brink of suicide and gave her *hope*. That elusive hope so many people desperately search for. Often they don't even know what they are looking for. To me, that's a greater miracle than most. That letter further illuminated the hand of God and the wonderful things He was doing. I will probably never know the full extent of what God did, but it's wonderful to know that Jason's short life had meaning that extends to eternity. Thank you, your story and others like it have been a blessing to my family and me.

Forever Changed

They say that hindsight is 20/20 and sometimes it probably is. On the other hand, foresight can be blurred, distorted, and often just outright wrong. Mine was definitely wrong and any vision I had conceived of the future was now in disarray. It's just natural for us to imagine how our children's lives will unfold, and I was no exception. So there was no way I could have foreseen one of my sons dying as a teenager. There was equally no way we could have predicted how the loss of a son would affect our lives. Unfortunately, after the commotion of the funeral died down, this reality is what we found ourselves staring straight into.

Somewhat to our relief, the week of Jason's memorial service passed by swiftly. There were still, of course, media inquiries and regular visits from many close friends. However, the intensity of the spotlight we had found ourselves thrust under was finally beginning to wane. Everyone was trying to return to his or her life. Our lives, of course, would never be "normal" again, though I wouldn't have considered our lives overly normal in the first place. But the gaping hole left by Jason's sudden and permanent departure ensured we would never see life again through the same eyes. One of the few positives of that week was that all of our remaining children were able to stay with us. They drew on us for support and we on them. It was also good to be able to keep an eye on them and see how they were coping with everything. Part of me was never worried as I trusted God, but the other part was in turmoil watching my family grieve. In the end, I was just glad they were there. It allowed me to be a father to them during a time when they needed it. Even more to the point, I think I needed it.

As the week ended, our eldest son, Jeff, and his family headed back to Calgary. However Mark, who had been living there as well, decided he felt God wanted him back in Taber, so he quit his job to move home. We were grateful to have him around the house again and I think it maybe helped fill the void a little.

Looking back at that time, there were some very interesting effects that the whole situation had on our lives. For Diane and me, one of the first noticeable alterations in our daily routine was that we just couldn't do basic chores. I mean we literally could not bring ourselves to do some of the chores we had done for years. This lingered for months and was interesting to say the least. For me, I just could not cut the grass. I mean really, it just seemed so ludicrous to spend time doing something so monumentally unimportant in light of losing our son. Therein lay the problem for me. I couldn't help but contrast everything in life against the background of Jason's death. It was in this all-revealing light that God really reminded me of how insignificant and hugely inconsequential most things in our civilized little lives are. I began to crave more than ever to concern myself only with things that had eternal impact. I pray that as you read this you will evaluate what you do with your time. Not that we should never cut the grass again, but we need to be careful how we spend our limited time. I had to relearn this lesson in the harshest of ways. Please don't wait for a permanent wake-up call like we received.

Thankfully, as the Lord carried me through this time of revelation and growth, a local landscaper offered to cut our grass for the rest of the year. I'm sure it was more of a blessing than he knew and I want to thank him for it. For Diane, it became an agonizing experience to cook meals. Di has never really enjoyed cooking even though she is very good at it. We had been blessed with a lot of donated food but eventually that ran out. She found it very difficult to get motivated to cook. So over the next few months, we ate a lot of meals at restaurants. These were really unexpected side effects of Jason's death, but they were only minor ones.

The primary change was wrapping our minds around the fact that Jason wasn't coming home – *ever*. It would seem a simple matter intellectually – it's quite logical and straightforward. If someone had asked me whether Jason was dead, I would have most assuredly responded yes. It would be quite the thing to have gotten that mixed up, such a tragic event. How could you not know or remember? However, our intellect and emotions are funny things. It was and is definitely not that simple. I often found myself passing by Jason's empty room and my brain would instantly start thinking, "Is Jason at home tonight or is he working?" There were several times I almost asked Di that question, but thank the Lord I caught myself in time. Occasionally even today I will see or smell something and instantly be reminded of him. For that moment it's like Jason is right there. My brain temporarily forgets that he's gone. Then suddenly and mercilessly I come crashing back to reality like an inebriated bull in a china shop. Those moments are sweet though. You can hear his voice and see his big smile as he heads out the door to work or school. And of course, there is still pain every time those moments end, my brain re-orienting itself with reality.

It's a funny little dance your emotions and mind do together. The mind is always in the lead and the emotions naïvely go wherever they're led, even when the mind detaches itself from reality. So, four years further down the road, my mind still isn't totally wrapped around Jason's death. And you know, I don't think it ever will be. That simple logical fact can be extremely elusive and a lot further from simple than you might realize. Nevertheless, caring family and friends, along with the grace of God, have allowed us to move on in a healthy way.

On the Road Again

There was another significant and very unexpected change that entered our lives shortly after Jason's death. I really thought that this particular change would be short lived. Instead, it has become more of a semipermanent transition in my life rather than a brief detour. You see, shortly after Jason's death, I began getting requests to be a speaker at many events. It started off fairly slowly, but by the summer I was inundated with requests for the fall. People wanted me to speak on television, radio, and to audiences in schools and churches. I didn't realize it right away, but it was all part of the plan God was weaving through this whole situation. He had planted the seeds for a travelling ministry during all the attention we received. Now He was beginning to water them.

Some four years later, that ministry has matured and evolved into quite the time-consuming call on my life. It's remarkable how God has orchestrated everything. He has opened some amazing doors and I have spoken in every province along with two of the three territories. He has taken me into all kinds of venues. Often He's led me into what would normally be hostile environments for a Christian speaker, and done amazing things. I have spoken in over two hundred schools (mostly public, some private, and some separate) where even the mention of Jesus would usually set the "politically correct" education system into a frenzy. I've spoken at antibullying conferences, teacher's conventions, safe school conferences, numerous prayer breakfasts (including the National Prayer Breakfast on Parliament Hill), restorative justice meetings, and an eclectic array of churches, town hall meetings, and more. I always let people know well ahead of time that I will be talking about what God has done. Almost always they have no problem with this. Many of these public events would never have even thought about inviting someone like me a few years ago.

For some reason, people often think that this travelling ministry is somehow glamorous. Maybe it's just me, but I have found it extremely draining and far from glamorous. I do, however, really enjoy meeting new people and seeing what God is doing around the nation. We have also had enough feedback to know that God has used these speaking engagements to touch many precious lives. This feedback really adds to my sense of peace about Jason because it reinforces the fact that he did not die in vain. There have been what seems to be an infinite amount of special moments during my travels, and I will try to share some of them here.

One of the first requests, if not the very first, came from a man named Mike Love. Mike is a Pentecostal pastor and he also happened to be in charge of YC, a large youth event. The event that year (1999) was being held in Red Deer, Alberta. I'm told there were some 7,000 young people in attendance. This was kind of a new thing for me. I had been to many conferences and events but usually not as a speaker. Now that I had received a few requests, I wasn't sure what to do. I'm not really sure what my hang-up was. It certainly wasn't the speaking, as my wife would vehemently confirm to you. So I stewed and then I prayed, stewed and prayed. Of course that is not the way I should have done it. I should have just prayed first, and then I would have had no reason to stew. Anyway, after several days of consideration I accepted the invitation.

YC was to be held during the May Victoria Day long weekend. So when the time arrived, Diane, Jeff, and I all made the trek to Red Deer. As we pulled up to the arena we could see that it was filled with young people, almost ready to burst at the seams. There was a Christian rock band on stage as we entered and you could sense the Lord's presence. We didn't have very long to look around before the staff ushered us off into the maze of artery-like hallways. Eventually they deposited us somewhere in the bowels of the building. Slowly we made our way to the backstage area. Peeking around the corner I saw what seemed to be an endless sea of people.

Before I knew it, Mike Love was introducing us and we were led onto the stage. I must say that at this point we were unprepared, surprised, and overwhelmed by the crowd's reaction to us. They gave us a thunderous standing ovation that we couldn't believe. Eventually they quieted down and Diane and I both spoke briefly. I really wanted to encourage these kids. I said that while evil had prematurely ended my son's life in an attempt to destroy our faith and family, he had miserably failed on both counts. Jason was now in Paradise with Jesus and so he did not get our son. On top of that, our family's faith had only been strengthened. It was a blessing to be able to speak faith to those young people. The place was absolutely electric and hung on every word.

As we finished and were about to leave the stage, to our surprise, Mike and some other people marched out with a 30-foot-long banner. It had some Scripture from Jeremiah 29:11 on it. "'For I know the plans I have for you,' declares the Lord, 'plans to prosper you and not to harm you, plans to give you hope and a future.'" (NIV) It was amazing because the whole thing was covered with thousands of signatures. Encouraging words and Scriptures were crammed on it, front and back from the students at YC. It was dedicated to the students of Myers High School. Standing there in the middle of 7,000 people and seeing this wonderful gift was powerful.

Upon returning home, banner in tow, I promptly headed over to the school. Once again, some of the staff seemed a little wary of my presence. But the principal consented and said that it could be displayed in the school. That banner was hung in the hallway where Jason was killed. It continued to illuminate that place with God's Word for the rest of that school year and through most of September the following term. Eventually we would end up with that banner. It still blows my mind that for many months this banner, covered with the Word of God, adorned the hallways of a public school.

Another of my first adventures with this brand new ministry would cover a whole lot more ground than our short jaunt to Red Deer. This trip was really the first significant travelling I would do. An old friend of my dad's from the '70s and '80s had contacted me. I hadn't seen him in over 20 years since I was fresh out of high school and plumbing with my dad. Ernie, a Christian, was now involved with an organization known as Campus Crusade for Christ. He invited me to a lunch meeting with three of the key people in that organization. This was the beginning of what would turn out to be a significant relationship.

At the meeting, they relayed their interest in having me speak at a series of events to be held across the nation. These events were called "Power to Change." You may have seen advertisements on television with professional athletes giving a bit of a testimony. This was a fairly significant campaign and the first place they would be visiting was the Maritimes. So they asked me to go there and speak in schools and to pastors in various communities.

That trip was to be my first time in the Atlantic provinces. It turned out to be quite the whirlwind tour of New Brunswick and Nova Scotia. And it was on this trip that I began to realize how draining an itinerant ministry could be. I was speaking up to six times a day, but thankfully I was travelling with a wonderful man of God, Barry Bowater. The pace was, to say the least, demanding, but it was well worth it. One of the first places I spoke was in the Fredericton High School. It was a large school, with some 2,700 students at that time. I had to speak twice because they couldn't get everyone into the gym at once. The silence was incredible during those talks. God's peace was literally blanketing the crowd and speaking to people's hearts. Barry was dumbfounded at the absolute silence for the duration of both assemblies. His background is in teaching and he couldn't believe how well the students listened and behaved. To be honest, neither could I, and we both knew God was doing something.

Amazingly, He has continued to move and this has become commonplace in most of my talks to schoolchildren. Often I've had teachers and principals come to me to comment on how their students have never been quiet before, no matter how serious the subject matter. I have given it much thought. I'm sure that some of the silence is because of Jason's story, but I also know that God has moved in each talk. There is a tangible holiness about the silence of the students that I can explain in no other way. These first two trips signalled the beginning of what has turned out to be a wonderful ministry. There are so many stories. So many lives God has touched.

I can still clearly remember speaking in Ottawa one time. I had been brought there by Focus on the Family to speak at one of their conferences. They had set up this wonderful opportunity for me to speak to the general public. God was most definitely at work that night. There were probably around 200 people who filed into the building that evening. The meeting began with some introductions and a presentation that shared the vision and work of Focus on the Family. Eventually I was called up and I spoke for around 40 minutes. There was the usual peaceful hush draped over the audience and a few tears rolling down a few cheeks.

After I finished, a small line of people began to navigate their way toward me. I spent time speaking to many of them. Then I noticed a middle-aged woman with a young man (her son) walking down the aisle toward me. As she approached, I could see the tears already welling up in her eyes. They were peaceful tears though, something I hadn't seen a lot of in my travels, and something I hope to see far more of in the future. She began to speak and told me the story of her other son. She shared how only a few weeks earlier she and her son had sat down to watch the video of the memorial service. The power of God had touched them both, and after the video was finished her son had decided to give his life to Jesus. Then she dropped the bombshell, explaining that only a handful of days later, he had died. Now I realized why there was peace behind those tears. We stood there, tears now filling my eyes, both of us sharply aware of the pain created by the death of a precious child. Both of us stood, also knowing the joy of their place in Paradise and that we would be with them again. Few words were spoken after this and they weren't needed. But looking back on that day my heart longs to see that familiar peace behind more of the tears I encounter on my travels. There will always be at least some pain in this life – there's no way to completely eliminate it. Our broken nature will make sure of that (though we can minimize it). But there can be peace even in your darkest days. I long for more people to know that peace, to know that joy.

Being launched into this itinerant ministry has allowed me to experience many new joys. The greatest, though, is seeing people around the country experience real forgiveness and encounter the one real God. There was one night in Swift Current, Saskatchewan, about a year after Jason's death, that comes vividly to mind. A youth missionary organization had invited me to come and share with them. One of the planned evenings was a public meeting. There were several hundred people present that night, and God once again graced us with His presence.

That night I simply shared our family's story, forgiveness being the main focus. After I finished, we extended an offer for people to come forward. They were welcome to come and just say, "Hi," or ask for prayer. One man caught my attention right away because he had an obvious look of distress on his face. He was in his early thirties and doing a very poor job of hiding his torment, though he sure seemed to be trying. It looked as if he was debating with himself whether or not to come forward. The tug of war must have subsided because eventually he did come.

He began by sharing a bit of his life story with me. It was a life full of challenges and hurts like many others. He elaborated on how the events of his life had conspired to lead him down a path of anger and bitterness. He had never realized how bound he was by this anger until that night during the talk. His eyes were finally seeing in a different light and he now clearly saw the burdens that weighed him down. He strongly expressed his desire for freedom from those chains. Forgiveness, he realized, was a concept badly needed in his life. He said that he had never asked Jesus to be Lord of his life, so I asked him if he'd like to do that. He nodded his head enthusiastically. I was able to lead him in a prayer of commitment, repentance, and forgiveness. Praise God!

It was a beautiful thing God had done once again. You could literally see his burden growing lighter. I never, ever grow weary of seeing the physical change in people as they are released from years of burden. It's not an exaggeration to say that this man's face was now almost beaming. He literally stood much more upright. I watched the mask of pain fall from his face and the hidden sorrow flee from his eyes. When we lay down our pride and let God truly touch our hardened hearts, real freedom is found, freedom found nowhere else.

There are probably as many frustrations that accompany this ministry as there are joys. But I must add that each joy far outweighs its counterpart. I think my biggest frustration is that it becomes very difficult, and often impossible, to follow up with the people you meet and minister to. In the fall of 1999, I was at a meeting in the Maritimes. There was a youth event at a church there and God did some wonderful things. It's a marvelous sight to see passionate young people fill a church. One young lady approached me, weeping. As tears cascaded down her face she told me a story, a horrible story.

Simply put, she had been sexually abused by some adults that she had trusted. My heart broke as she told me and I struggled with my anger. Anger that people can hurt one another so maliciously and so callously. I did what I could in such a short time frame. I shared with her the healing freedom that forgiveness could bring and then prayed with her. I also let her know that it can take time to arrive at a place of letting go and forgiving. For her own well-being, though, she needed to find that place with God's help. Even after such a terrible wrong had been done, forgiveness is the only place she would find freedom and be able to move on.

Because I can't personally follow up with situations like this, I often spend much time in prayer for the people with whom I have spoken and prayed. I ask the Lord to send others into their lives to support them. It is still disconcerting, though – so many people pour out their hearts and hurts and then you have to leave. There is only so much you can do in a matter of minutes or hours. I know that God is using this ministry to initiate the healing process in many, and therefore has plans on how to finish it. He's a big God after all. It's in

His hands and there's no better place for it to be, but I still wish I could get updates sometimes.

Of course, not every circumstance is dramatic. I don't want to paint an unrealistic picture. But I have always seen God sovereignly move in each talk – maybe not dramatically, but He is always impacting people. There was a teachers' convention in the Shaw Centre in Edmonton. The Lord allowed for a time when people could come forward after the talk (as is quite common). Several people lined up and I remember talking with a woman. Out of the corner of my eye, I saw a man who was passing swiftly by veer toward us. He snuck in just as the lady had finished, leaned in towards me, pursed his lips and simply said, "I just wanted you to know that after listening to your talk, I gave up a grudge I had held since 1970." It wasn't dramatic or incredible in a worldly sense, but what a powerful victory for that man in a spiritual sense. When bondages like that are broken, they *are* just as powerful and miraculous as when God heals someone of cancer. Because, in fact, a spiritual cancer has been healed and removed and that is often more difficult than healing physical illnesses. All too often we don't understand the power we have witnessed. We only see with our fleshly eyes. We need to remove the scales from our spiritual eyes. We must begin to see how serious many of these spiritual problems are, instead of just reacting when they dramatically manifest in the physical world in the form of violence, addictions, etc.

Another powerful, yet not so plainly visible, event took place in London, Ontario. I was speaking in many venues on another whirlwind tour of Eastern Canada. After having spoken in one of the high schools there, a wonderful story was relayed to me. A young man had gone home from the talk and promptly sat down with his parents for a two-hour discussion. This is an all-too-familiar situation in our Western society today. There was virtually no communication between him and his parents. Thankfully he decided to change that.

Later in that trip, the vice-principal from a Roman Catholic school imparted to me another story. Apparently after my talk, God had touched several hearts and the most prominent bully in the school had inquired if there could be a meeting arranged. This wasn't any normal meeting he wanted to set up – it was a meeting so that all the kids who were being picked on could share how they felt. Talk about God moving mountains! What an incredible thing to hear. God really moved during that trip, as He faithfully always does.

There was also an evening meeting called "Youth for Christ" near the end of that London trip. A young girl approached me and told me that she had not been able to attend the talk I had given at her school. She wanted me to know that afterward at least a dozen of her non-Christian friends had sought her out. They all began asking questions about her faith. It's these encounters that rejuvenate me when I'm weary of the travel. As long as there is a chance that even one person may be impacted, I know that it is well worth it. I feel very blessed and privileged that God called me to this ministry. Many times He has used the Christians I encounter while travelling to bless me and to minister to me when my tank seems to be running on empty. I only pray that I can continue to be faithful to His call, and I wish to thank everyone I've come in contact with on these travels.

I will share one last story that, for me, puts everything into perspective, and makes it more clear why I continue to travel. I was in Calgary walking down the hall of a large high school. Two students who had been assigned as my hosts were ushering me along. I had just finished speaking at two large assemblies and was on my way out. One of the young men looked over at me and began talking.

He said, "I consider myself a realist." This was his way of telling me he didn't believe in God. "But," he said energetically, "I had never thought before about the possibility of having a relationship with God. I am going to have to find out more about that." I looked at him and encouraged him to do just that. I told him to seek after truth and to seek after God. This story is the epitome of why I travel. You see, when all is said and done, this is what life is all about – a relationship with the Creator of *all*. I am so thankful that I was in that relationship on the day Jason died. God gave us the grace to walk through it and to continue walking today. My relationship with Jesus has been, and continues to be, a place of healing and strength. There truly is no other place to go!

You know, I never expected all this attention, and I definitely never expected it to last. But here I am years after my son's death, and I continue to pray that I would only do what God calls me to do. Trying my best to do nothing out of ego, but only out of my desire to honour and be obedient to the Lord.

The Shooter

By this point I'm sure that many of you are asking the same question. What about the shooter? What happened to him and why did he do it? I'm not sure that I can satisfactorily answer all of those questions, but I will pass along what I do know. I also want you to know that I will be referring to him as "the shooter," not because this is how I see him, but because he was and is a young offender and names are out of the question. Regardless, for the sake of clarity, calling him "the shooter" seemed to be the simple answer to a difficult problem. You see I don't view him simply as the murderer of my son. On the contrary, he is a young man made in the image of God. Albeit he is a very broken and hurting young man, but he is far from alone in this. In spite of what some people might think, he has value and a destiny. Most importantly I see him as a person whom God loves intensely, regardless of what he's done. So you see I want it to be clear that he is much more than just "the shooter," and I hope my use of the term doesn't lead you to that perspective.

Since everything has happened, Diane and I have had the opportunity to speak with the mother of the shooter. We have also talked with many of the shooter's acquaintances and had the privilege of getting to know one of his friends. This has allowed us to learn some of the history of this young man's already tragic life. I think it rather important to understand some of this basic history so we can learn from it.

Various factors conspired to alter and shape the shooter's life. The first of these factors was that he lived in a broken home. I use that term because in counselling many families through divorce there is always pain, even when divorce is an absolute necessity. My intention in bringing this up is not to condemn anyone who has gone through divorce. But we must see how damaging it can be, so we can seek the healing that is necessary and avoid so many broken families in the future.

Whatever you want to call it, when the family structure that God has created is ravaged by divorce there are many visible wounds, and even more invisible wounds. We often don't understand the depth of the spiritual connections between us. In Genesis 2:24 it says:

> *For this reason **a man** will leave his father and mother and be united to **his wife**, and they will become **one flesh**.* (NIV, emphasis mine)

When a man and woman enter into marriage there is a spiritual *fusion* that takes place. Likewise, there is also a deep spiritual connection between children and their parents. We have all heard of the "bonding" that goes on between a mother and her newborn child. Well this concept is much deeper than most of us realize. As well, the father also has a deep "bond" with his children. This connection between people can be very positive (as was intended by God) but also very negative. It is also what I call the "open door" between members of a family unit. This is why parents are so influential in their kids' lives. It is also the source of the deepest and most invisible wounds. Just think about your own life for a minute. If you're walking down the street and someone calls you a nasty name, that can seriously hurt. But, if your dad or mom attacks you verbally, it hurts exponentially more. There is that open door between you and your parents. So, when the stranger attacked you it didn't penetrate as deeply. Attacks from your family go right through the open door. Not only are you emotionally hurt, but you are also wounded on a spiritual level. Please be aware that I'm using a fairly healthy example of a family unit. If you are attacked repeatedly by your family, the relationship will be somewhat more closed. However, the connection is still there.

In the family structure, parents were intended by God to protect and provide for their children. Alongside this they should also teach their children how to act and behave. When you consider how deeply united children are with their parents, you may begin to understand how deeply these lessons become embedded. Thus, parents can pour into their children values and morals (among other things) in a way that no one else can. It's amazing when you begin to realize that God created families to be in unity with one another on the deepest level. But, we must also realize that when this unit is damaged it affects every person on that deep level. This is why divorce is so devastating.

My plan here is not to write a whole section on how families can be healed. There are many good books that deal directly with this issue. However, we must begin to teach our children how important the family unit is. We must begin to understand the spiritual connections that are created between us. (On a side note, this spiritual fusion that takes place between men and women is one of the main reasons God tells us not to have premarital sex. It's not that He wants to deprive us of pleasure; after all He created sex. But He understood that when we sleep with someone a spiritual connection is created. Outside of marriage it can be very detrimental. If you go sleeping around with different people, just think of the spiritual ramifications. God's desire is to protect us and keep us healthy. He will even heal us and break ungodly spiritual connections if we come to Him.)

Many people today enter into marriage as if it were temporary. They have a nonchalant attitude about the *covenant* of marriage. We must recapture our understanding of how important it really is. It is not to be taken lightly and it is important enough to sacrifice our own desires for. If we begin to bring God into the centre of our relationships, rather than ourselves, the divorce rate would drop immensely. For anyone who is already divorced please take heart, there is hope. God can and does heal even the deepest wounds. But, we must be aware of these deep invisible wounds before we can ask God to heal them. Once more I would like to reiterate that I am not condemning anyone who is, or has been, divorced. But, the fact remains that the shooter in our story came from a broken family and was deeply wounded when this occurred. Not only were his parents divorced, but his father lived on the other side of the country. His friends often heard him mention how he missed not seeing his father more regularly. There is no doubt that this played a pertinent role as one of the many factors that set him on his destructive road.

The second factor that I feel was very significant in the shooter's life was bullying. He was just one of those kids who was a prime target to be picked on. He endured several years of taunting and bullying at the hands of several peers. The years of torment obviously took their toll. As previously discussed, the wounding from peers is different from the family. Nevertheless the wounding from this sort of prolonged and drawn-out abuse is extremely damaging, on all levels. No one deserves to go through that kind of abuse. And, no one can escape being wounded by that kind of abuse either.

It is the shooter's wounded spirit that I would like to focus on. Through divorce and bullying (among other things of course) this young man ended up with a very wounded spirit. The emotional manifestations of a wounded spirit can be very painful and destructive (i.e., depression, anger, rage/hatred, self-hate, etc.). Unfortunately most of us don't recognize the spiritual root of the pain and so we seek answers that never get beyond the surface. As the pain builds and lingers it can begin to dominate our thinking and feeling. There are many people out there with wounded spirits. Some people are obviously more wounded than others, but you'd be surprised at how many are wounded and don't even know it. We get so used to living with these wounds, that eventually we're not even aware of how our thought patterns have become programmed around them.

I believe the shooter in this case became so overwhelmed by this pain that he could contain it no longer. We also know that the shooting at Columbine High School in Colorado mesmerized him and this drove him even more. Driven by pain-induced anger he reached a breaking point and without the loving touch of Jesus, there was no relief from this boy's pain. The deep healing his wounded spirit desperately cried out for was not found. Only God can heal the really deep hurts in our lives. We must submit to Him and His touch if we wish to see people like this shooter helped before it is too late.

Another factor substantially added fuel to this fire and warrants mentioning. If you look under the surface of this boy's life you will see the footprints of evil at every corner. No, I'm not saying the shooter was evil. The evil I'm talking about is something most of us sedately dismiss and/or ignore. As a Christian I have a relationship with God, I know He exists. But, if God exists then we must also understand that the devil exists as well. This is spiritual evil I'm talking about here. Unfortunately most of us have seen one too many Hollywood versions of evil to take it seriously anymore. We see evil as something to laugh at; it doesn't really exist. We consider ourselves too intelligent to be duped by old wives' tales. Our culture tells us if we can't see, taste, touch, or understand it, then it is not real. Sadly for us, just because we've bought into this lie doesn't mean we are right. (Please note that I'm not saying Hollywood's version of evil is terribly accurate, but that doesn't necessarily negate its existence either.) I believe that every time this young man was wounded, evil was right there to capitalize. It helped stir this young man's rage, and even exploited the Columbine tragedy to fascinate and stir him towards its goal. At the very least it spurred him on toward this terrible catastrophe. The shooter had had enough and was going to do something about it.

I have been asked several times whether my son Jason knew the shooter. Some have even suggested that maybe Jason bullied him and that's why he was shot. Well let me put that to rest here and now. I can tell you that I knew my son, and though he wasn't perfect, he was a kind-hearted young man who did not bully other kids. I can also tell you that according to all his friends, many general acquaintances and teachers, Jason was not a bully and had never met the shooter. To add to this further, the shooter's mother told us personally that he didn't know whom he was shooting. It seems that Jason and his friends were simply in the wrong place at the wrong time.

So what did happen to the shooter? It took quite a while for his case to come to trial, partly because of the log-jammed system, but also because he had some health problems. While in custody he had a stroke (due to a defect present from birth) and it affected the blood flow to his brain. Sadly there was some permanent damage done. After he recovered from this incident the case finally proceeded.

Diane and I never attended the trial; we just didn't see any need. I've often seen people in similar situations attend the trial diligently, saying they needed to find closure. From our point of view, we had forgiven this young man and seeing him punished wasn't what he needed. We simply wanted, and today still want, to see him get the help he needs. I want to get a phone call one day saying that the shooter has found Jesus. Besides, no matter what punishment someone can receive, it would never bring the victim back. There is no closure in the punishment of the perpetrator; only through forgiveness will the wounds begin to heal.

Even though we didn't attend it, the prosecutor in the case kept our family updated on the events of the trial. They decided not to move it to adult court and the shooter was eventually found guilty. He was sentenced to three years in the juvenile detention system. Two years after the trial ended his mother moved back to Ontario and had the shooter transferred to a centre in that province. Even as you read this book he is probably out of the juvenile system by now. I pray for him often, and hope he never ventures down another path so catastrophic. I've often wished I could meet him face to face and forgive him directly, maybe explain to him why we forgave him. Unfortunately we have never been given the opportunity, but maybe we will in the future. Either way my family and I will continue praying for him, and we know God answers prayer.

Canada and the Future

Wake-Up Call

For me, Jason's death led to a large web of questions. Everywhere I go, invariably someone asks what my son's death meant. I will do my best to answer some of those questions here. What Jason's death did for me was to magnify and bring into clear focus some very important questions. I think we have to start by asking what did Jason's murder (or any murder for that fact) really show us about this wonderful country we call home? What has gone wrong in this wonderful, wealthy country of Canada? What has to change and how do we facilitate that change? These questions are the key to understanding where we are and where we're headed.

I can't count the number of people who have told me they believe Jason's death was a significant wake-up call to the nation. They say that this country of ours is going seriously wrong and there need to be some momentous changes. I can't claim ignorance to this line of thinking and odds are that you can't either. As a Christian pastor, it was no revelation to me that the country was headed in a deadly direction. I've known for years that much of the ethical and moral thrust of our society was navigating in ungodly streams of thinking. The foul odour from these streams has been wafting for a long time and, as I said, I can't claim ignorance. I've also known that these kinds of societal currents rarely bring anything but destruction and damage. Perhaps it is easier for me to define how I see Canada by using the very lens I see through – the Word of God.

In Galatians 6:7,8 Paul clearly illustrates the eternal struggle for all people and nations of the earth:

> *Do not be deceived: God cannot be mocked. A man reaps what he sows. The one who sows to please his sinful nature, from that nature will reap destruction; the one who sows to please the Spirit, from the Spirit will reap eternal life.* (NIV)

I have watched many changes occur in this country over the last thirty years, many of them not good. Canada was built on Biblical morals and foundations. And now, with a simple inspection through that same lens, we can see how far we have strayed from our foundation. Without strong moral foundations this country will collapse just as Rome once did. The problem with this statement is that I have *watched* many changes occur and not done enough about them. About five months after Jason's death I was in Halifax, Nova Scotia, doing a radio interview. There came a point in the interview when this man asked a question that I had not been asked before. To be quite honest it really caught me off guard.

He asked, "So who is responsible for your son's death? Who do we blame?" I remember having to hesitate, and think very carefully how to answer that loaded question. Finally I responded by saying this: "Well, if you want to talk about who is responsible for Jason's death, I will be the first one to step up and take some responsibility." Waves of surprise and shock flooded the man's face as I answered. I went on to explain that I had seen all of these changes forging their way into our society. While I knew they would bring destruction and chaos I had for far too long been a *quiet*, respectable Christian. I can no longer be silent, so I will now try to share over the next few pages what I believe has gone wrong and what the solution is.

The Moral Decay

In general, I think we are now seeing the visible manifestation of deep-seated societal problems – all of which are focused on the fact that the very moral fabric with which our society is woven has begun to unravel. History has taught, time and again, that whenever we move away from the moral foundations God has laid out, we bring death on ourselves. I do not have the time with this book to take an exhaustive look at all the contributing factors to this moral erosion. However, I will mention a few of the key issues that face us today.

The first thing we must look at is the myriad of challenges that wealth brings. Very few civilizations in history have experienced the kind of peace and prosperity that North America has enjoyed since World War II. We are in a somewhat unique situation and, along with the blessings this has brought, there are many basic realities and problems we seem to misunderstand. Even when we do understand them, we do little to change them.

The first effect that wealth seems to bring is the intense desire to increase our status or to keep our position. At all costs we will fight to keep our comfort zones intact. The sweet juices of luxury known by the majority of people in Canada have created an extremely internally focused people. (That includes almost everyone – even the lower middle class live what is in reality a very comfortable life.) We have become a people who will often whine at the slightest suggestion that we may lose even a small fraction of our comfort. Think about it for a minute. The most common gripes people have with the government all focus on perceived threats to our incredibly high standard of living. Governments spend enormous amounts of money and energy to project an image that takes credit for increases in our comfort, and shifts blame for decreases. This is simply because there is obviously nothing more important to the Canadian people at this time.

Out of this arises a people so blinded by their perceived need for comfort and material things, that we often choose to ignore obvious problems, fearing we may lose the benefits of our comfort. We are a people who have no wish to rock the boat because we falsely believe this comfort provides happiness; so we don't speak up even when things are going terribly wrong. We fail to realize that the trouble out on the street is only a heartbeat away from our doorsteps. I believe I have come to profoundly understand this truth in the murder of our son. Our little town of Taber is one of the most unlikely places to ever have a school shooting. Even after Columbine, I still would never have believed it. *Then it happened.* When Jason and our youngest son, Matthew, went on a mission trip to Tijuana, Mexico, many things happened. It was all new to them, but do you know what surprised them the most? Those poverty-stricken people of Tijuana were happy – the kids were all happy too! They couldn't understand how these people were happy when they had nothing. No homes, toys, nothing. They had to struggle just to find food each day. We have to understand that material objects/wealth are not the bearers of happiness. We've got to realize this and stop taking the "bury-our-heads-in-the-sand" approach. We need to stop trying to protect our wealth because it's not all it's cracked up to be. Frankly, the harder we try to protect it, the more certain our eventual loss of it becomes. If we keep ignoring the realities going on around us, we will pay an increasingly higher price. We need to ask ourselves, how much is our imagined comfort zone worth? Is it worth the loss of human life? The first challenge I bring to us, then, is to understand that we can't remain silent when things are going wrong, no matter what our reasons.

Not only do we think that wealth brings happiness, but we also seem to think that the value of people or a nation is measured with the same ruler. Consider a pickup truck, for example. A pickup truck is designed to carry a maximum payload. If we continue to put into that truck more than it is designed to carry, we will eventually do permanent damage and even destroy the truck. The Roman Empire was wealthy, too, but as it drifted far from its moral foundations, it came to a crashing halt. Why? Because it overloaded its pickup truck! You see, God is the Creator and Designer of humanity. He has given us a precise set of blueprints to live by. This is not some sort of punishment, nor does He desire to take all the fun out of life. On the contrary, God knows exactly how we were designed. He knows our needs and He loves us so much that He has given us guidelines to live by. These shouldn't be viewed as restrictions. These guidelines are there to protect us, so we can live life to the maximum without destroying ourselves in the process. If we would set aside our pursuit of wealth and pursue God, we would find peace, joy, and the richest life possible. We would also be changed from a self-seeking, self-centred people to a more loving and giving people. We would measure our value by our moral identity, rather than by our material wealth.

The Instant Gratification Revolution

Let's go back in time for a minute. Imagine you are part of a family in the first couple of years of the twentieth century. You live on the Prairies in a modest house nestled next to the side of a hill. It's a bright, sunny day with no clouds in the sky and there's a gentle summer breeze caressing your face. You look out over your fields of wheat, locked in a dance with the wind, their golden-brown sheen is pleasant to the eye. The smell of supper cooking in the house wafts to your nostrils, mmmm, fresh-made bread. You look out on the horizon. What do you see? No cars, no paved roads, no power poles, no power lines, no telephone lines, not even any fences for that matter. Just wide-open undisturbed country – an endless horizon that seems to stretch to the end of the earth. The silence is deafening, and then you feel an odd vibration on your side. It's just your beeper going off, nothing to worry about. Hold it, there weren't any beepers in the early part of the century.

147

That's right, this idyllic scene is completely undisturbed by modern-day technology. I'm sure this is relatively unfathomable in today's technologically crazy generation. You probably couldn't even make it through that little daydream without some form of technology bothering you. Whether it was a call on your cell phone, or that nagging thought that you'd better check your e-mail. You see, our society has arrived at an incredibly unprecedented time in history. There has never been a society before that has, or could even imagine what we have. It's what I call *the instant gratification revolution* and has resulted in a terrible increase in selfishness.

I can't see another time in human history where a society enjoyed the ability to instantly gratify virtually every whim or want. We enjoy instant communication through the television and Internet. These same mediums bring us instant entertainment. We have fast food and high-speed transportation that can take us around the world in a matter of hours. You can walk into a store and buy anything you need and almost anything you want. With the benefit of credit we can buy homes, vacations, and just about anything our little hearts desire. Skillfully navigating this gluttonous sea are, of course, the advertising agencies. They have helped create a people driven by their desire to have more, and more, and more!

There has been an incredible shift in people's attitudes fueled by this technological surge. My children's generation has grown up expecting to get whatever it wants, whenever it wants it. An attitude has developed that says, "I deserve it, and I will have it now!" Whenever circumstances challenge this assumption, the volcano of anger that erupts from people is quite disturbing. We must understand that this reality has impacted everyone, including you and me, whether we realize it or not. To generalize, I would say that it has made us less courteous people and has led to an increase in violent behaviour. Have you ever wondered what road rage is all about?

Let me give you a couple of examples of this effect on our lives. Virtually all of us experience the pressure of not having enough time to accomplish everything. Picture yourself rushing into a grocery store on your way home from work. You are running very late and there are important things that you *must* do at home. You only need a couple of items so you rush from one side of the store to the other (of course the items you need are always on opposite sides of the store). Having attained your coveted items, you head briskly toward what the store laughingly calls the "express aisle." You know the one I'm talking about, where it says nine items or less. I really don't know why they have these lines. My experience tells me they always put the slowest check-out people on them. Just as you are approaching the back of the line a shopping cart appears out of nowhere and beats you there. You furl your brow, thinking to yourself that it is never good when someone enters the express line with a *cart*.

Time is passing and you are getting later and later. Standing in line, you begin to peek over the shoulder of the person with the cart. You start to count how many items are actually there (come on, don't kid yourself, we all do these types of things). So, you're there counting and it dawns on you that they have more than the maximum allowed nine items. How are you feeling at this point? For many of us, anxiety is immediately beginning to assert itself. I watched this very scenario unfold one day, and the man in front of me asked a lady with a cart to move to another line. You see, we have become such an agenda-centred people in our high-pressure world, that anything or anyone who gets in our way angers us – often more deeply and more quickly than we are aware of.

Here's one more example of how things can so easily get out of hand, straight from my own life. A few years ago, I went into a fast-food restaurant to grab a quick meal. It was the height of their lunch rush and there were two lines at the counter. I seem to have a special gift of being able to always pick the slower line – it works every time. So, as is usual, I picked the slower line not realizing it. Not long after I had arrived in line, someone came into the restaurant and stood in the line beside me. Before long this person had moved up and, of course, I hadn't. My immediate thought was, "Hey, this isn't right. I was here first and that guy is now ahead of me."

Before long that guy was all the way up to the counter and I was still mired three people back in line. Watching this guy walk by with his food was the straw that broke the proverbial camel's back. I began to think of the comments I should make to the person serving my line, if I ever got to the front. Due to the crowded restaurant, and coupled with the many employees scurrying around behind the counter, I really had no idea who was serving my line. Either way I was sure ready to give them a piece of my mind. At last the glorious moment came when the person in front of me walked off with her food. I would now be able to vent my self-centred frustration. There standing in front of me was a teenage girl. She was a small person with big glasses and she had that "deer in the headlights" kind of look. Beads of sweat profusely adorned her forehead. Across the vest pocket of her uniform and the brim of her hat, written in large yellow letters was the word, *trainee*. I stood there looking at this poor, overwhelmed girl and said nothing. I made no comment other than to order my food and say thank you. As I sat down, I began to ponder what had just happened. I realized that for the sake of about five minutes, maybe less, I had been prepared to hurt another person. All because I had not received my fast food as *fast* as I thought I should. As I sat there pondering, it seemed so silly to me. I realized that in my grandparents' day there was no such thing as fast food – most meals took hours to prepare. We get caught up in our little worlds so much that if someone gets in the way, we are willing to just run them over with our anger. In extreme cases, people cross the line from verbal expression to physical aggression, road rage being a prime example.

One of the principles that God really impressed upon Diane and me after Jason's death was that we had to become people-centred instead of agenda-centred. Daily, we put our busyness ahead of living, breathing people. My daughter made this painfully clear to me a few weeks after our tragedy. She was seven at the time and found me pecking away at the computer in my study. Like many seven year olds, she could often be found drawing and colouring. She entered the office proudly showing off her latest creation. "See what I did, Daddy?"

Without even looking away from the computer or stopping my typing I said, "Yes Jen, that's nice." She turned and walked out of the room. As she disappeared around the corner I thought, *what did I just do?* I had sent an unspoken message to my little girl that my work was more important than she was. Thankfully, she returned a short while later with another creation. This time I gave her my full attention and her face lit up as she skipped away.

I don't believe it's easy to become people-centred again. I'm not naïve. There has been significant chaos from time to time in my life, generated simply by putting people ahead of my schedule. But I have done and continue to do my best to stop my agenda whenever possible for people who are in need. It isn't easy, but it is totally worth it. Whenever you stop your agenda for someone, a subconscious message is received: "This person must really care because they gave me some of *their time*, and I must count because this person seems to value me." I would not even begin to boast that I am any different than anybody else. I know the only reason I have been able to begin moving away from this selfishness is Jesus. Only He can take you to that place of true freedom, where you can truly care about other people and desire the best for them. So my second challenge is for us to become people-focused instead of agenda-focused. I believe that if we all began moving in this direction, we would be astonished at the immediate changes in all aspects of society. Being people-centred fosters an environment of patience and care. Agendas tend to make us impatient and quickly angered, just like I was in the fast-food restaurant.

Violence as Entertainment

Unfortunately, I must start this section by reminding us all that violent entertainment is by no means a new phenomenon. For example, the elite of Rome were entertained by inhumane and barbaric acts of violence in the coliseum. Sadly, as we have grown and progressed through human history, we have been unable to eliminate this from our forms of amusement. There have been many studies and books on this issue, and it is not my intention to discuss this in great detail. However, in the big picture, it is a significant part. So I will briefly examine this issue to reveal my next challenge to us.

The first and most obvious point is the disturbingly subtle way in which we seem to become desensitized to the whole issue. It's a simple fact of life that as we are exposed to something over and over, we become used to it or comfortable with it. In other words, we become numb. If something was initially shocking to us, after a while it will totally lose its shock value. Think of a horror movie. I know several people who enjoy this form of entertainment. At first, I think, they liked the thrill. These movies scared them, made them jump in their seats. But after years of watching them, there is no longer anything (no matter how grotesque) that can shock them. I don't even know why they like these movies any longer because they have seen nothing really new or innovative in quite some time. The point is that they are now comfortable with the most shockingly violent things. Their compassion for people in pain has become dangerously eroded without them realizing it. That's the key. They don't even realize how detached they've become from reality.

A few years ago there was a book entitled *Stop Teaching Our Kids to Kill.* Lt. Colonel Grossman, a retired psychologist from the United States military, authored it. The premise of this book was that many of the violent video games that are popular with young people today are just variations of videos that were developed by the U.S. military to train soldiers how to shoot and kill. Think about this for a minute. These are the same tools the military is using to train its soldiers (and probably, for that matter, desensitizing them so they can kill when needed). There is a generation of young people out there practically being raised by television and video games – often because their parents are too busy working, or pursuing something else. I don't know about you, but this is more than just disturbing, in my opinion.

I had the opportunity to listen to Lt. Colonel Grossman in Calgary a few years ago. He shared some more unsettling information at that time. One study he referred to was particularly pointed. It was a study of foreign countries where American television had been allowed to be a part of daily life. In every single case, fifteen years after the introduction of American programming, the rate of violent crimes had doubled. The premise was that once a generation had grown up with U.S. television, they were twice as violent as the preceding generation. I'm not prepared to pin everything on television, but maybe we should really start asking ourselves some questions. Just how much does our entertainment change our attitudes? How desensitized have we become?

In Edmonton, Alberta, a couple of years ago, two teenagers beat an acquaintance one Saturday afternoon. Their reasoning is irrelevant because there is really no excuse to harm others. But the point is that they left this kid where he fell, unconscious on the ground. A few hours later when they returned, he was still there, unconscious. They promptly proceeded to kick him some more. Sadly this young man died of his injuries two weeks later. The two teens were charged with murder. This story is absolutely horrifying and we need to realize that the victim could have been anyone's kid, maybe yours! What made me even sicker to my stomach was that the young man had been so badly beaten they couldn't identify him at first. We need to ask ourselves, what has happened to the mind of a Canadian teenager? How can anyone treat another like that? How could they possibly think that this treatment of another human being was needed and/or justified? How do our kids come to the point where this is seen as some sort of a solution to their differences? Perhaps it was just entertaining to watch another bleed and suffer. This should be a serious wake-up call. Sadly, it doesn't seem to bother people the way it should. We need to see the big picture. So it wasn't your kid. But it could have been, and it could be, next time. Violence is so prevalent in Canada today that we can no longer pass it off as only a few isolated incidents. There is obviously a wider problem that's affecting people everywhere and we must look at it.

More food for thought came my way from two of Jason's best friends, three days after he'd been killed. They were hanging out with a group of teenagers in Taber. One of them happened to be from another school in town. They were talking about what had happened and just life in general. The teen from the other school piped up and shared his feelings. He said, "I thought the worst thing about the shooting was the fact that it didn't happen in my school, because I didn't get the extra three days off from school." How do young people become so insensitive? Let's ponder this for a moment. If he's that desensitized to murder, how far is he from carrying it out himself? If murder seemed to be a solution to his problems, it scares me to think how dangerous kids like that are. It doesn't take much to push them past that line because they're desensitized to it already. Again this brings us to the question: Is violence really the kind of entertainment that we should be feeding ourselves? Or our kids?

Second is the specific message our entertainment seems to be sending. The theme of revenge seems to me a common thread in the tapestry of societal amusement. Not long ago, I sat down and watched a number of television shows during a week at home. I decided to focus primarily on sitcoms. Now the theme of revenge is obviously a common thing in action movies, but it's not always associated with comedy. However, without exception, revenge was in every show. Many times it was the main motivation for the plot of that particular episode. The dangerous thing about this is that these shows are designed to make us laugh, and so it seems all very harmless. But there is one question that continues to nag me. If our children watch show after show, developed around the idea of getting even with someone, how can they not get the message that this is how you deal with life's problems? I believe that this is exactly the message they receive and understand.

I was in northern British Columbia speaking at a school a while ago. A student approached me after the talk, and asked if she could share a story with me. I obliged and she began to share an all-too-familiar story. She told of how another girl in her school believed that her best friend was interested in this girl's boyfriend. Her answer to this perceived threat was to gather three of her friends and beat up the problem. The victim spent a week in the hospital nursing her wounds. I was so sorry to hear this story, and it again reminded me that revenge is almost a way of life for many young people. I'm so tired of hearing or reading about stories of revenge.

My third challenge to us then is two-fold. We need to begin to take accountability for what we allow our children to use/watch as entertainment. Second, we need to begin to speak up against these trends that have swept our nation. We must set the example for our kids that revenge is not a solution.

Childhood, What Childhood?

The last point I want to touch on is closely tied in with the previous challenge, and it is extremely pivotal for the course on which we seem to be headed. Simply put, it is the diminishing of childhood. No one can deny the fact that we have given our children access to more and more adult information. The things on prime time television today would have been absolutely scandalous a couple of decades ago. I really can't figure out why we have done this, and I certainly don't know how we expect our children to be able to handle it. Adults are negatively affected by most of this stuff, so why would we think our kids wouldn't be?

I remember going to all four of my sons' first "sex ed" presentations when they each reached grade five. Sadly, there were only one or two other parents there besides me. The presentation was in the form of a video, and gave a very basic understanding of human reproduction. As I watched each of my sons in this situation, it was obvious to me that without exception, they weren't at all interested in the presentation. I believe they weren't ready for the information, and I still haven't figured out whose bright idea it was to implement "sex ed" at such an early age. Why do we insist on diminishing the years of innocence for our children? I do realize they grow up eventually, but it seems to be damaging when it is stolen too early. When my daughter was in grade three, she made the comment that several of her classmates were allowed to watch

"R" rated videos at home. There is good reason movies are rated "R" and no child should be exposed to that. Today many elementary school girls seem to be interested in make-up, boys, and the latest bare navel pop star. Shouldn't they be using their imaginations or playing with dolls at this age? How sad it is that we have removed the *peace* of innocence from our children at earlier and earlier ages. Children are by no means ready to understand adult concepts, and their twisted interpretations are almost always damaging. My last challenge to us then is to protect our children and leave their innocence intact.

There are many issues that impact people today, but I believe many of them are spawned from similar roots. Far too often we have allowed those in society with the more dominant personalities and loud voices to dictate social currents. They have told us that basically no one has any right to prevent people from doing virtually anything they want to. Behind this is a deceptive spirit that uses the media to broadcast itself and has deluded the nation. We foolishly think we are being kind and generous and *open-minded*, when in reality we are destroying ourselves. This same spirit spends every waking moment attempting to convince everyone how loving and tolerant it is. And yet, as soon as someone disagrees, its true colours arise and it labels the dissenter close-minded or a bigot. Look at the issues that ravage our nation today. The pornography epidemic, abortion laws, and the euthanasia debate, to name just a few. This open-minded thinking has led us to view people more as objects. We see them as objects that are there for our use, and far too often, our *abuse*. This is the exact opposite of where we thought we were heading. We're so loving, aren't we?

Yes, we need to do everything in love, but there is a huge difference between love and tolerance. Often really loving someone means doing the hard thing, taking the difficult stance. Truth is often very hard to accept, but it is truth, and people can *not* do whatever they want. We need to stand up and let people know where they're headed. They need to know the truth even if they don't like it. God is not mocked. We will bring destruction on ourselves if we aren't prepared to stand up and be counted, speaking for what is right.

In Genesis chapter 1 we are told that God created men and women in His image. This gives us insight into who we *really* are. We are made for relationship with the Creator of the universe and with each other. God created us and He loves each and every one of us, even those whom we think are unlovable. Why do we think some are better than others? We don't have the right to put others down. Indeed, Jesus teaches us that we actually have a *responsibility* to care for and honour each other. When we look at other people we can't be seeing objects – we have to see a person precious in God's sight. And maybe, if they are precious in God's sight, they should be precious in our sight as well! There is an old adage that floats around the church – we are to love people and use things. It must be grievous to our Heavenly Father to see how much we do it the other way around.

Life makes no sense at all without God. Why should we care about people? If we are just evolutionary accidents, what difference does it make how we treat each other? Outside of self-preservation (eye for an eye) there is no reason to have compassion for others. Of course, none of us can escape the fact that the "Creator of all there is" built into our hearts the intense and insatiable desire to love and be loved. This is the place we must come to, the place where we learn to honour and have compassion for each other. Knowing the love of God and spreading that love around is the only real answer. Breaking the cycle of being hurt, becoming angry, and then looking for revenge (often we call it justice) will only be accomplished by the grace of God living in us, so we can forgive and thereby demonstrate true love.

I would also like to point out that the challenges we have looked at are by no means meant to be a comprehensive list. Rather, they are meant more as a magnifying glass that might cause each of us to examine more deeply the reality of our lives. A place for us to start affecting change is in this nation of Canada. It is on our heads. We need to begin to take accountability for our silence and speak out. We need to be accountable as parents, and protect the future generations from our mistakes.

What Tomorrow Brings

We live in amazing times and I believe we will soon see incredible changes in the way many things are today. As we boldly pioneer into the twenty-first century, we are straying further and further from the moral track. Change is imminent, there is no denying that. Yes, we can bury our heads in the sand and ignore the obvious chaos around us. Or we can be part of what God is doing. Everywhere I look in the Christian world there are two things happening. The first is that many Christian churches are almost indistinguishable from the world. We have created a cultural Christianity that costs us nothing, and seems to be no more than a mix of worldly morals and religious tradition. A Christianity where we have Jesus on our terms, instead of making Him Lord of our lives (a direct result of our self-centred drive for more). A Christianity that is almost completely lacking the supernatural. Many Christians know nothing of spiritual giftings and are indeed afraid of them. On the other hand, I see that God is doing a new thing. I believe He is preparing the nets for the endtime harvest. Emerging is a bold Christianity that is radically obedient and primarily about sharing the tangible love of Christ. A Christianity that makes Jesus Lord of everything and has relationship with the truth. An intimate, passionate love affair with the Creator of all. A Christianity that walks in a spirit of faith, that believes without seeing. A supernatural Christianity that moves in the giftings God has given us from the inception of the Church. God is calling us to stop "playing church" and start following Him.

The world is, of course, heading down the opposite path, and seems to get darker almost weekly (and this is exactly why we must be a radically obedient and servile church). When we survey the moral horizon of our own nation, we see an indisputable move away from Biblical values. We have arrived at a place described earlier where people believe that whatever they choose to indulge in, short of murder, is their business and therefore must be allowed. We have placed this premise under the umbrella of individual rights. The question that strikes me is, what happens when the rights of two individuals clash? Who wins? No matter what people say, at some point the basic needs of society as a whole need to be considered. Each individual's choices *do* impact everyone else in the country. I'll give you an easy illustration that I've noticed in certain stores. Often because of the proliferation of, and hunger for, pornography, I have noticed it is now displayed in some public grocery stores where my ten-year-old daughter may go to purchase a soft drink. This is not even close to being OK, and we shouldn't be allowing it to happen in our nation. I have no doubt that the words of Paul in Galatians 6:7,8 apply to our current condition:

Do not be deceived: God cannot be mocked. A man reaps what he sows. The one who sows to please his sinful nature, from that nature will reap destruction; the one who sows to please the Spirit, from the Spirit will reap eternal life. (NIV)

There is little doubt that Canada has sown to please the sinful nature, and I believe we are seeing the results all around us. I do believe that my son's death was a wake-up call to this reality, but it is far from being the only one. We need only look as far as September 11, 2001 to understand that things need to change. Punishing criminals does not solve problems. It is simply an attempt to alleviate symptoms. If we are not ready for a turnaround in our values and the way we live life, we will continue to reap the disaster we are sowing. Our jails won't be big enough to hold all the criminals, and graves won't be numerous enough to hold all the victims. My heart breaks at the thought of all the pain and suffering we are headed for. In this comfortable life we live, it is too easy to ignore God and His desire for our lives. Personally, I would prefer to see things turn around and ignite revival across this land. The other alternative is that something drastic will happen to force us out of our comfort zones and into a place where this nation will seek Him, rather than ignore Him.

There is a key question we must ask in all of this: Is the Church ready? Are Christians prepared to be part of real, radical Christianity or have we become so ensnared by our comfort that we are unwilling to change? Would we really rather continue to have strict religiosity (like the Pharisees in the Bible) and/or cultural Christianity than to have a deep, life-changing relationship with God? This is not an easy question to ask and it is perhaps even harder to be really honest with ourselves about the answer. It is imperative that we examine our relationship with God. If this does not challenge you, then perhaps you need to ask if you're being honest with yourself. If you don't think that you have played church at some point, then you're probably not being honest again, or you're just unaware. We have all been affected by these things, including myself – but it is not too late and there is so much more God has planned for each one of us.

The remainder of the text in Galatians 6 carries on in verse 9 by saying: "Let us not become weary in doing good, for at the proper time we will reap a harvest if we do not give up." (NIV) The promise is clear and exciting. If we are willing to persevere and pay the price of being obedient to Him, we will see a harvest. It is the cry of my heart to see that harvest, when countless numbers of people will come to know the life-changing, radical love of the Lord, and in turn, will set this nation on fire for God. None of us individually can turn the direction of this nation around, but all of us walking in Biblical unity with the power of the Holy Spirit will see the transformation of this country. How could we not hunger for such a time? A time when drug dealers go out of business because no one needs such poison to escape life. A day when you realize that the porno shops have all disappeared. Once Jesus touches hearts and lives, we will then see transformation on our streets. How amazing would it be to have practically empty jails? Many people think this is simply impossible, a pipe dream at best. I say that is good news because God specializes in the business of doing the impossible. Canada has a destiny, and it's not to collapse from the inside out, as we seem to be doing presently! Are we ready? Are we willing? What lies ahead is exciting and it won't be easy, but we must learn to engage and enjoy the battle!